ON THE WAY
TO BETHLEHEM

On the Way to Bethlehem
An Advent Study

On the Way to Bethlehem

978-1-7910-3328-6

978-1-7910-3330-9 *eBook*

On the Way to Bethlehem: DVD

978-1-7910-3332-3

On the Way to Bethlehem: Leader Guide

978-1-7910-3329-3

978-1-7910-3331-6 *eBook*

ON THE WAY TO
BETHLEHEM

AN ADVENT STUDY

ROB FUQUAY

Abingdon Press | Nashville

On the Way to Bethlehem
An Advent Study

978-1-7910-3328-6

MANUFACTURED IN THE UNITED STATES OF AMERICA

To my grandson,
Geronimo Delise,
whose birth and young life
remind me of the words
of Carl Sandburg,
"A baby is God's opinion
that the world should go on."

CONTENTS

INTRODUCTION

A trek to the base camp of Everest. That is what I chose for my sabbatical. I am preparing for that trip as I write this book. Friends ask why I didn't choose to go to a beach and read some books. That answer would be too much of a detour. For now, let me just say that preparing for such a journey as to Everest Base Camp requires a lot.

My wife is joining me in the expedition. We will travel with a group and recently we had a meeting with some of our fellow trekkers. I found out quickly how behind I was in reading all the materials sent to us by our guiding company. Someone mentioned the challenge of keeping all our belongings to the thirty-three-pound limit. I said, "That's not right. Airlines allow luggage to be fifty pounds per bag." It was clear I hadn't read the manual.

Each person has to carry their own water along with what they want to have with them while hiking, but porters carry all other belongings. Those bags cannot exceed thirty-three pounds. Then there was information about the precise kind of shoes we needed to have. There were also recommendations on correct clothing to wear, items we need in case we get sick, gadgets for keeping phones charged. No, there's probably not much cell reception in the Himalayas, but if we use cameras to take pictures, then we need a battery-powered charger.

There was information on cultural awareness dos and don'ts. The ability to purify water is the responsibility of each trekker. We need to prepare for having Nepalese currency in order to tip our sherpas. We must have certain insurance in case of emergency evacuation. Yikes! Needless to say, I was more apprehensive about the trip than I was before this meeting, but mostly because of how unprepared I was.

Any important journey requires preparation. Even trips not as complicated as a trek to the base camp of Everest take preparation and planning. How will we travel? Will we break up the trip along the way? If so, where will we stay? What will be our route? What kind of weather should we expect? What clothing should we have? Will we need travel documents, other currency, inoculations?

For many people, the anticipation of a journey is half the fun. Doing all this work builds excitement about the places you will see and the experiences you hope to have. One thing is for certain, we never return from a journey the same. Our journeys shape us. We learn from them. We form and deepen relationships along the way. We have unexpected encounters that move us and provide memories that last the rest of our lives. Some journeys even change our lives.

It is no wonder that the word journey is used as a metaphor for the spiritual life. From beginning to end, the Bible is a collection of journeys. God called Abraham to leave his home in the land of Ur of the Chaldeans and make his way to a place God would show him. That call and his response set Abraham on a path that led to the land of Canaan and his becoming the father of a nation to be set apart for God. Islam, Judaism, and Christianity trace their histories back to that journey.

Moses led the Israelites out of Egypt into the wilderness where they journeyed for forty years. Those years were fraught with life-threatening obstacles and life-altering decisions, but along the way they came to discover the character of God and God's plans for them.

The residents of Jerusalem journeyed to Babylon defeated and hopeless, but a generation later they would journey back to Jerusalem with new hope and a new desire to live faithfully.

The disciples journeyed with Jesus throughout Israel for three years. During this time, they experienced miracles and heard teachings beyond their understanding. They became a tight-knit community. They gave their lives to continuing the ministry of Jesus.

The apostle Paul journeyed throughout the Mediterranean world starting churches and spreading the good news of Jesus Christ. In his lifetime, he traveled roughly ten thousand miles. His journey took the church beyond the boundaries of Judaism and brought hope to people of various nations, races, and languages.

The Bible ends by picturing a new heaven and earth, reminding us that when this life ends, all life doesn't end. The journey continues, and there are more adventures that await.

Many of us associate the Christmas season with traveling, but have you ever thought of Christmas as a journey? The same is true in a spiritual sense. Advent is the first season of the Christian year. We begin the year moving toward Christmas with themes like preparation, getting ready, and waiting as if we're going on a trip. The difference, however, is not to get to *a* destination but to destinations. We find the meaning of Christmas throughout this journey. As the old saying goes, the journey is the destination. This is the way to Christmas.

This book explores the spiritual meaning of the important locations in the Christmas story. Each chapter begins with several pages offering descriptions of the featured locations. We start in Rome. This may seem an odd place to include on a journey to Christmas, but the birth story in Luke 2 begins by mentioning Caesar Augustus. A decision made in Rome is what led to a birth in Bethlehem. Without Rome we don't have the Christmas story as we know it.

In Rome you are invited to consider the longings you have for your life and our world. Sometimes we carry longings we don't fully realize. We haven't put words to them. Yet these longings shape the journey of our lives. Identifying our longings and what they have to do with God and God's longings for us and our world begin to make this journey a life-changing one.

From Rome, we continue to Jerusalem where an elderly priest is having a once-in-a-lifetime experience. Zechariah and Elizabeth discover they are going to have a baby even though they are long past the hope and reality of doing so. Their son will be John the Baptist, the forerunner of Jesus. In Jerusalem, we consider the role that waiting plays in faith. The very city itself, and specifically the site of the Temple, on which now stands one of the most sacred Muslim shrines in the world, represents a history of people bringing their longings to God and then waiting. This waiting, however, is grounded in faithful remembrance of what God has done. Jerusalem invites us to consider what we do with our longings. What is it we wait for God to do, and how do we fold that waiting into faithful activity? Sometimes we discover that waiting itself is a gift.

After Jerusalem, we head north, to Nazareth. Some trips don't follow a straight line! But any journey to Christmas would be incomplete without a stop in Nazareth where a young girl in a most insignificant place welcomes an invitation from the angel Gabriel that will change her life and the world. Nazareth causes us to reflect on the value of simplicity. If we are not careful, any journey might cause us

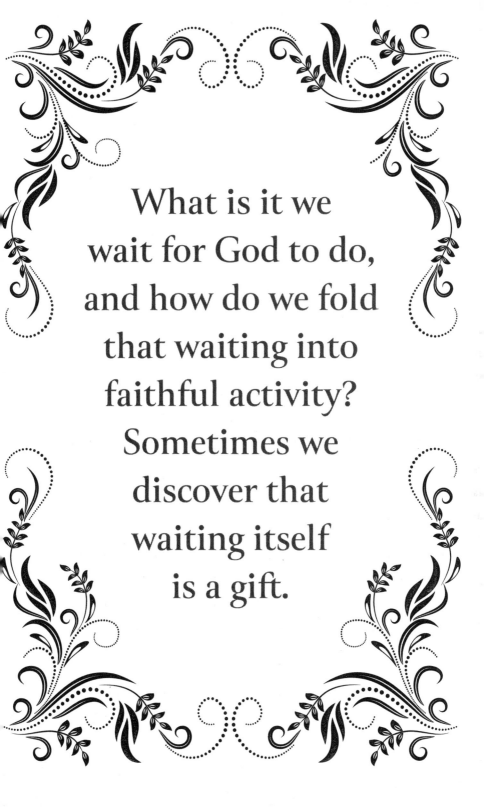

What is it we
wait for God to do,
and how do we fold
that waiting into
faithful activity?
Sometimes we
discover that
waiting itself
is a gift.

to obsess on schedules and where we need to be by when. Nazareth invites us to slow down and become aware of blessings we can't predict. Every trip yields unexpected benefits. Nazareth may even be a place to repack our bags and consider if there are some things we no longer need for our journey. We learn to travel light when we choose to stop carrying things that don't enhance our journey.

Finally, we end up in Bethlehem, the completion of our way to Christmas. This location may be the most familiar to you, but don't assume you know your way around. There may be some things to learn about Bethlehem that give a new understanding to the meaning of Christmas and why this journey is worth taking. Bethlehem teaches us humility, and this may be the most impactful visit on the way to Christmas, one that leaves us like the wise men, going home a different way.

In the epilogue we visit Persia, a place of return, the home of the magi who visit Jesus in the Gospel of Matthew. There we consider the idea of return and the way a journey changes us. We arrive home different from when we started, just as the magi leave Bethlehem and journey home by another road. The return is as important as the journey.

What we gain from all these places will be different for each person, and different even for ourselves over time. If we took this same journey every year, what we gain from it would not be the same, because we change. God speaks to us where we are, and where we are this Advent is different from any Advent in our lives.

That may be a good place to start our journey, considering some questions that help us assess our individual starting points. What is different about you this year from any year prior? What has changed? What are things you are facing you never have before? How would you describe your faith compared to a year ago? Five years ago? Ten years ago? Think of these questions as choosing which suitcase you want to use to pack for a trip. These questions will hold what you carry through this season and shape the meaning Christmas has for you this year.

Consider sharing this trip. Journeys are more impactful (and safer!) when we travel with others. If you are in a small group using this resource, bring your full self to the discussions. Be vulnerable. Sometimes we can't know what we think until we speak. Groups help us find clarity and richer appreciation for the sights we see. As the African proverb goes, "If you want to go fast, go alone. If you want to go far, go together."

Finally, think about rhythms you can add to your journey. As you read, perhaps keep a journal close by to write down thoughts that come to you. Maybe they are questions, or actions to take. Writing down these inspirations will increase the likelihood of acting on them and prevent the journey from ending with the last page.

Also, build a time of prayer into your schedule. You might consider having a quiet time to center yourself before reading. In fact, you might think about not reading this book straight through. Spread it across a weekly routine through Advent. Take time to reflect on each chapter and what the different locations mean to you. Use the scriptures referenced in the chapters for separate reading and reflection. Keep a prayer list of people, celebrations, needs you want to bring before God. Take time to be still and welcome God into your thoughts. This will be like acclimating for higher elevations and allow your soul to breathe deeper.

So let me offer this prayer as you begin your way to Christmas:

Dear Lord, may I become more aware this season of the journey of my life. Help me to see and discover you as my Guide. As I make my way to Christmas, may I step aside from the daily destinations of life to consider where my journey is ultimately taking me and where you want to lead me. Help me to be open to sights and stops you want to show me as I go, so that when I arrive at Christmas, I will be at a new starting point of my journey. Amen.

CHAPTER 1
ROME
A Place of Longing

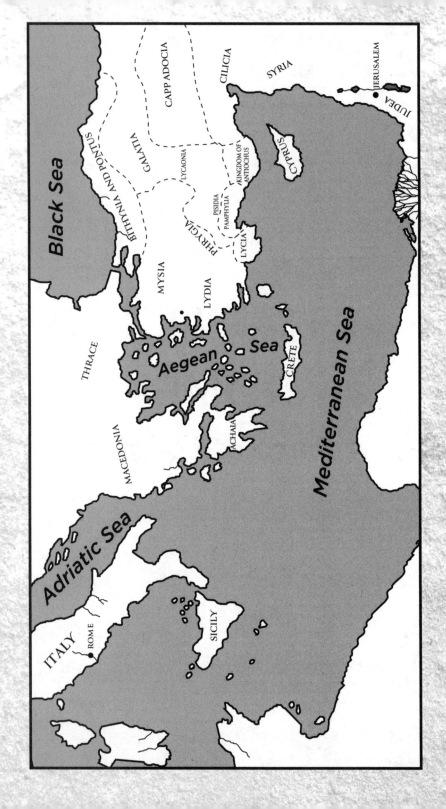

Introduction to Rome

Rome is the capital of Italy with a population of nearly 3 million people and covering an area close to five hundred square miles. It has the largest metropolitan population in Europe with roughly 4.5 million people. Often called "The City of Seven Hills," Rome is located along the Tiber River in the central region of Italy and is the only city in the world to have a country unto its own within the city limits, Vatican City.

The seat of the Roman Catholic Church, Vatican City is ruled by the pope, also known as the Bishop of Rome. The center of Vatican City is the magnificent St. Peter's Basilica in which the remains of the apostle Peter, the first bishop of Rome, are believed to be buried beneath the altar. First built in the fourth century, the present church was reconstructed in the early 1500s under Pope Julius II. The need for finances to build the church led the pope to intensify fundraising practices like the use of indulgences, slips of paper church members could buy assuring their forgiveness of sin. Such practices stoked the resistance of people like Martin Luther who led the Protestant Reformation. Yet for any appearance of opulence and grandiosity, the number of churches, religious statues, and icons point to Rome's Christian history and how it also came to be known as "The Eternal City."

Rome is also full of ancient ruins, such as the famous Colosseum, recalling times when gladiatorial games were held there. Slaves, known as gladiators, were forced to fight for their lives as entertainment for crowds. Historians estimate that the Colosseum could hold fifty to ninety thousand people, rivaling the size of modern stadiums and arenas.

This period also highlights Rome's political influence in establishing principles that shaped much of modern democracy. Founded in the eighth century BC, Rome was one of the first cities at the time to have an electoral monarchy, a ruler chosen by the people. By the sixth century BC, Rome was governed by a republic, with elected officials known as senators who worked with the ruling monarchs. Following the civil wars, Octavian emerged as the leader, taking a title from the last name of his great uncle, Julius Caesar. Calling himself Caesar Augustus, he came to power in 27 BC and thus began the Roman Empire.

Augustus founded the two-hundred-year period of Roman peace known as the *Pax Romana*. He extended the Empire through much of Europe, the Middle East and north Africa. During this time the city of Rome flourished. The population is estimated to have been around a million people, making it the largest city in the world at the time. By extending the size of the Empire, Augustus built roughly fifty thousand miles of highways. The most famous roads of ancient Rome were the Via Ignatia and the Via Appia. Augustus is credited for ordering several censuses, often for the purpose of increasing tax revenues for the Empire in order to support its expanding military, aqueducts, and roadways. One such census was taken around 6 BC and is believed to be the cause of Mary and Joseph having to travel to Bethlehem to be registered.

CHAPTER 1
ROME
A Place of Longing

In those days a decree went out from Caesar Augustus that all the world should be registered. This was the first registration and was taken while Quirinius was governor of Syria. All went to their own towns to be registered.

Luke 2:1-3

I consider that the sufferings of this present time are not worth comparing with the glory about to be revealed to us. For the creation waits with eager longing for the revealing of the children of God, for the creation was subjected to futility, not of its own will, but by the will of the one who subjected it, in hope that the creation itself will be set free from its enslavement to decay and will obtain the freedom of the glory of the children of God. We know that the whole creation has been groaning together as it suffers together the pains of labor, and not only the creation, but we ourselves, who have the first fruits of the Spirit, groan inwardly while we wait for adoption, the redemption of our bodies. For in hope we were saved. Now hope that is seen is not hope, for who hopes for what one already sees? But if we hope for what we do not see, we wait for it with patience.

Romans 8:18-25

I remember my first Christmas away from home. I was twenty-two years old and in my second year of seminary. Jim Ridgway Sr., the founder of Educational Opportunities, created a trip for seminary students. During the month of Christmas break, students could study and travel in the Holy Land with renowned biblical archaeologist Jim Fleming. I jumped at the chance.

About fifty students from various denominations stayed at the Jerusalem Center for Biblical Studies. We were from all over the country. I ended up palling around with three other guys who were as eager to learn as I was. Dr. Fleming made clear that what we got out of this experience was up to us. If we wanted to learn as much as we could, then stay close. Whenever the bus pulled up at an archaeological site, and as soon as he stepped off the bus, he would start walking and talking. If we were there to relax and enjoy the surroundings that was fine. Walk at your leisure, but if you wanted to learn, keep up with him. The four of us were usually the first off the bus each time.

A few days before Christmas we were traveling back to Jerusalem through Bethlehem. The bus stopped in the town, and Dr. Fleming explained we could have a little time to shop for souvenirs. That region was a different place in 1985 than what it is today. There was no West Bank wall. Travel between Jewish and Palestinian areas was less restricted.

The four of us walked the narrow streets of Bethlehem, occasionally stepping into a shop to peruse the popular olive wood carvings. In one store we met the owner, a Palestinian Christian named Ahmad. When he learned that we were seminary students and wouldn't be home for Christmas he said, "If you happen to come back to Bethlehem on Christmas Eve, be sure to come by my shop. My mother makes chicken and rice. Celebrate Christmas with me."

As we left, we jokingly said to each other, "That has to be the best marketing line anyone has ever used!" We were skeptical to say the least.

A few days later, on Christmas Eve, we finished our work in time to catch a taxi for Bethlehem. We were quickly disabused of whatever sacred and holy experiences we had imagined. A barrier had been erected around Nativity Square. It got this name because of the main building facing the square, the Church of the Nativity, built over the site believed to be the place where Jesus was born. We had to go through an intense search to enter the square. The area was heavily populated with soldiers carrying machine guns. The tension was palpable.

Once inside, we experienced a sudden jolt in atmospheric conditions. The mood was more akin to New Orleans at Mardi Gras. Okay, maybe that's a bit much, but folks were there to party for sure. We found an open table at an outdoor café and listened to international choirs singing Christmas songs from a makeshift stage built beside the church. We were starting to regroup. We said, "Can you believe it? We're in Bethlehem on Christmas Eve!"

About that moment a scuffle broke out beside our table between two Palestinian youths. Immediately several Israeli soldiers surrounded them and began beating them with the butts of their rifles until they were motionless on the ground. They dragged them away leaving a small trail of blood. We sat in silence for a good two minutes. One member of our group asked, "Do you guys just want to go back?" We all nodded and got up to leave. What we thought was going to be a place of sentimental spiritual meaning turned out to be a disappointment.

I share that memory to invite you to consider if Bethlehem might have looked similar on the night Jesus was born. Sure, we picture everything much differently. A quiet, moonlit sky. Candlelight in a stable with cattle lowing and baby Jesus cooing on a bed of straw. We sing, "O little town of Bethlehem, how still we see thee lie," but would it have really been that still?

Certainly, soldiers would have been present. A Roman census had been mandated. People had to return to their ancestral homes to be registered. The small village would have been overcrowded, many people no doubt irritated by the inconvenience of leaving homes and work some distance away. Crowded conditions and bad moods are not usually a good mix.

Plus, no one besides the locals would have been there by choice. Not even the soldiers. Everyone was there by decree, an order from Caesar Augustus that all the world should be enrolled. Strangers and friends alike would have wondered why. A census was usually taken for the benefit of taxes. Tax revenues were often considered by a leader who was planning for some sort of military campaign. Could all this be leading to war?

Apprehension, resentment, fear, weariness. These would have most likely described the mood of Bethlehem that first Christmas Day. These were the circumstances into which Jesus was born. No available housing meant Jesus was born in a stable. Some homes kept the animals in a room inside the house. Even if this was the kind of stable where Jesus was born, it was still a less than desirable setting. What caused Mary and Joseph to be in Bethlehem at such an inopportune time? Why did they make a journey of a hundred miles from Nazareth to Bethlehem? It was, of course, because of a decision that was made more than a thousand miles away. Caesar Augustus issued a decree. The Christmas story began in Rome.

Rome, Then and Now

We will come back to Bethlehem in chapter 4. That is the destination of our journey, but I begin by reflecting on my experience there in order to point out how the political and cultural environment that determined the conditions of Bethlehem in 1985 was a result of decisions and resolutions made in other places much farther away, in places with the power to determine what happens in a town like Bethlehem. The same was true at the birth of Jesus. The place of power that determined the atmosphere of Bethlehem at the time of Jesus's birth was Rome. Rome shaped the culture, the laws, and even the beliefs of people of other nations, races, and religions. Rome was the kind of place that could be referred to as if it were a person: "If Rome chooses this...if Rome doesn't figure something out...Rome must act now."

Rome was the center of the major Empire that wrapped around the Mediterranean Sea, as far north as Great Britain, as far east as Germania down through Greece and modern-day Turkey, and as far south as North Africa. Rome expanded on the city-state structure of Greek society forming a platform of government that looked roughly similar to modern American democracy. A senate balanced the authority of the emperor. Modern social services like plumbing, water supply aqueducts, engineering advancements in construction, and roadways spread through Europe, North Africa, and Asia Minor. Many roads and highways in these regions today are built over the networks created during the Roman Empire.

Rome came to rule in Israel after General Pompey captured Jerusalem in 63 BC. A strong military presence was a feature of Roman occupation. At the same time, Rome ruled through local client-kings, individuals of some recognized authority who vowed allegiance to

Rome and obedience to Roman law. This gave the appearance that Rome was genuinely a welcomed authority, but in reality, such client-kings were considered traitors to their own people. Many of these local authorities abused their power. Such were the Herods.

Herod the Great was the first member of his family to be granted the title of king. Though Jewish by birth, Herod spent a good bit of his early life in Gentile company. He ran in elite circles among the hierarchy of the Roman-political world. His association and alignment with Marc Antony and Octavian, who hunted down the assassins of Julius Caesar, would prove advantageous for Herod. Octavius became Caesar Augustus. In return for his support to Augustus, Herod was rewarded with the title king of Judea, an appointment approved by the Roman Senate.

Herod stopped at nothing to eliminate any threat to his position. Underline the word any. He executed his wife, his in-laws, and three of his sons. Alluding to Herod's quasi-Jewish faith, Caesar once remarked, "It is safer to be one of Herod's pigs than one of his family." (Remember, pork was not kosher.) So, the idea of Herod ordering the execution of male babies in Bethlehem because he learned a future king had been born there was not out of character.

At this point let's make a few observations about Rome. It is a place that has power to do good things. By creating aqueducts and sewer systems, disease and sickness were reduced. A military presence brought a certain amount of security and reduced crime. The Roman Empire was known for its advanced highways creating faster connection between cities in the Empire. Massive construction projects created jobs and stimulated economies.

But not everything about Roman occupation was good. While allowing certain freedoms for residents in occupied countries, compliance with Roman law was nonnegotiable. Those who broke the law were often punished publicly to serve as a warning to others. Crucifixion was a painful, humiliating way to die with crosses placed along highways. Bodies might be left for days to deter others from crossing Roman justice.

Rome also turned a blind eye to the injustices of leaders like Herod. For instance, Herod feared there would not be mourning when he died, so he gave an order that upon his death soldiers were to execute leading men of respect in Jericho (where he had a palace) to make sure there would be tears at his funeral. Rome had power to stop such things from happening but chose not to act. I suppose as long as taxes were paid and valuable commodities were being imported and exported, unfortunate events could be overlooked.

Then there was the lack of sensitivity to local religious convictions. One example is the requirement of Israelites to pay Roman tax. A special coin was used for the tax that had the image of the emperor on it with the inscription, "Caesar is God." This coin was a form of idolatry to Jews, but not paying was not an option. Another notorious example of disregard for cultural values happened right after Pontius Pilate was appointed by the Emperor Tiberius as prefect over Judea in AD 26. Immediately Pilate showed his willingness to provoke the Jews by placing standards with Tiberius's image on them throughout Jerusalem, an act of disrespect and disregard for Jewish faith.

Rome treated conquered people as second-class citizens, or perhaps more realistically, noncitizens. They had no vote or voice. What happened in Rome could adversely affect an individual's life, but there wasn't much that could be done about it. Although, the Jews did understand the power of politics. In the case of Pilate's placement of standards (banners), a delegation of religious leaders went to Pilate's headquarters in Caesarea to protest. Pilate surrounded them with soldiers who drew their swords, threatening to kill them if they didn't leave. The Jews lay down and bared their necks as if to say, "Go ahead!" They knew Pilate could not politically afford to have that much innocent blood on his hands in his first week in office!

Stories like this point out what had been building since Pompey captured Jerusalem. The relationship between Jews and Romans was contentious at best. The *Pax Romana* started under Augustus brought unprecedented peace and prosperity to Roman citizens, but for occupied lands like Israel the experience was different. The news that a decree had been made calling for a census would have been met with skepticism and cynicism by the Jews. They would have wondered if it would lead to higher taxes or the possibility of war in their region. Rome was not to be trusted.

What represents Rome for you? In the United States this might be Washington, DC, or your state capital or your county seat. Rome is that place where decisions impact your life beyond your control. Such decisions might be laws that affect your health-care coverage, access to public services, or the conditions of your neighborhoods.

Several members of the church I serve are part of a group in Indianapolis called the Rethink Coalition. They are examining ways to redesign the congested, somewhat unsafe section of highway in the inner city connecting I-65 and I-70. By and large, the interstate highway system created by the federal government under President Eisenhower in the 1950s has been a great asset to anyone who has driven long trips across the country. Designed for the military in times of national crisis, the interstate highway system has provided a high-speed network from shore to shore and border to border.

However, the downside of this creation was what happened in urban areas where highways were constructed right through

Rome is
that place
where decisions
impact your
life beyond
your control.

neighborhoods, often populated by poorer, underprivileged communities. People without much voice or power to change decisions made far away experienced their neighborhoods being torn apart. Friends and family were displaced to new locations. Compensations for their homes were often far below the values they needed to move to new neighborhoods. I have learned much from this group that is concerned with making road systems smoother but also doing what they can to heal injustices of the past so as not to repeat them.

Some of us live in Rome. We are in positions to make decisions that affect people far from us, and we must keep their needs in mind. But all of us live affected by the Romes of our world. We are all impacted by events beyond our control. Sometimes the impact is minimal, but other times it is deep and painful.

Think of a Ukrainian mother trying to keep her children safe because a decision was made in Moscow to annex her country. Or a family facing eviction because a property management company in a faraway city decided to increase their rent. Or someone you know losing a job because a decision was reached at the company headquarters to restructure.

Rome is that place where a stroke of a pen, a boardroom vote, a rap of a gavel, or an idea floated can launch ripples that become crashing waves on our doorsteps. When is the last time you were affected by some decree in Rome? What are the places in your life where decisions made far away had huge ramifications for you?

Rome reminds us of the reality of the Israelites. They lived under an occupying force beyond their control. They longed for more. They longed for freedom. They longed for justice. They longed for peace. But changing the way things were felt impossible. All they could do was long for something better.

This is where Advent begins, in longing. The way to Christmas starts in Rome, the seat of power and principalities where our hopes and fears are released and sometimes collide. A single leader's worries can manufacture panic among the rank and file. When King Herod, a ruthless, spiritually bankrupt leader in Jerusalem, learned that an infant king had been born in his region, the Bible says, "he was frightened, *and all Jerusalem with him*" (Matthew 2:3). The fears of people in power pull others into the vortex of their anxiety.

The journey to Christmas begins in longing, but not little longings. Not longings like New Year's resolutions: lose ten pounds, save more money, eat better. Rather, the longings of Advent are deeper and spiritual. What longings do you bring into Advent? That is a good question to spend time considering. Is there a longing to find a mate and fill a void caused by loneliness? Is there a longing to fill a void of loneliness *within* a relationship? Have you longed to have a baby? A safe place to live? Be reunited with a loved one?

The other side of this question is to consider the longings of God. What does God long for our world? This question can radically change the direction of our lives because when our hearts break over the things that break God's heart, God may call us to be solutions to the problems.

Maybe your heart gets disturbed over the lack of peace in our world. Wars and violence steal the lives of thousands each year. According to the Gun Violence Archive more than 118 people are killed by gun violence every day in the United States. There were well over six hundred mass shootings in 2023.[1] Perhaps you are troubled about mental health needs. More than fifty thousand Americans died by suicide in 2023, the most of any year in history.[2] As you pray and ask about God's longings for our world, will you become troubled about adequate health care, education equity, safe and affordable housing, climate change, or something else?

What comes to you may feel large and beyond your ability to change, but stick with it. Keep listening, because God doesn't reveal God's will to people without making a way.

What significant spiritual leaders haven't felt inadequate to challenge the Romes of our world? God said to Moses on Mt. Sinai, 'I am sending you to Pharaoh to bring my people, the Israelites, out of Egypt.'" But Moses said to God, 'Who am I that I should go to Pharaoh and bring the Israelites out of Egypt?'" (Exodus 3:10-11)

God said to Gideon, "'Deliver Israel from the hand of Midian; I hereby commission you.' [Gideon] responded, 'But, sir, how can I deliver Israel?'" (Judges 6:14-15).

God told Jeremiah, "I appointed you a prophet to the nations," but Jeremiah replied, "I do not know how to speak for I am only a boy" (Jeremiah 1:5-6).

God didn't show these servants *how* they would change the world. God simply gave them a vision of a changed world, then promised they would have God's company.

Dr. Martin Luther King Jr. was a modern prophet to be sure. His courage, intellect, and ability to inspire people rank among an elite few. But would we have ever heard of Martin Luther King Jr. if it hadn't been for Rosa Parks, who courageously refused to give up her seat in the whites-only section of a Montgomery city bus? Her subsequent arrest inspired the black clergy leaders of Montgomery to come together. They elected their newest member, Dr. King, as their leader and the civil rights movement was born. But would we have ever heard of Rosa Parks were it not for Claudette Colvin?

Do you know her story? Claudette was a member of Rosa Park's youth group. Exactly one month before Rosa Parks refused to change seats on a bus, a fifteen-year-old girl named Claudette Colvin did the same. The bus driver stopped and ordered her to move. When she didn't, the police came on the bus, kicked her, dragged her off, and took her to the police station and put her in jail. She later said, "Worried or not, I felt proud. I had stood up for our rights. I had done something not many adults had done."

Her pastor came and picked her up to take her home. On the way he said, "Claudette, I'm so proud of you. Everyone prays for freedom. We've all been praying and praying. But you're different. You want your answer the next morning. And I think you just brought the revolution to Montgomery."[3] Rosa Parks said it was the action of Claudette Colvin that inspired her action. You could say the civil rights movement began with the courageous resistance of a fifteen-year-old girl.

Most of the radical revolutions in history have started with the troubled spirits of individuals who long for a better world, individuals who usually feel inadequate to be change agents but who act upon their troubling. The two most significant ingredients for change are courage and trust. We must have the courage to let God trouble us in the first place. We must have the courage to believe that the purpose of faith is not just to comfort the afflicted but to afflict the comfortable. Then we must trust that God empowers us and works through our faithful actions. As John Wesley famously said, "Give me one hundred preachers who fear nothing but sin, and desire nothing but God, and I care not a straw whether they be clergymen or laymen; such alone will shake the gates of hell and set up the kingdom of heaven on Earth."[4]

What fuels such courage and trust is an immutable faith in God's active work in the world. By the time we see convincing evidence of God's activity, the heavy lifting by God has been done. Just think of a rain shower. Long before we see droplets fall and puddles of water form in our gardens, a process of evaporation has occurred. Water from the earth's surface reforms into unseen vapors that rise through the atmosphere gathering into something we eventually see, rain clouds! Long before there are visible signs, there has been invisible activity. The same is true of God.

God Is Always Directing

Let's return to the Christmas story and the journey that starts in Rome. This was long before satellites and instant messaging. By the time a decision was made in Rome, it could take months, if not a year or more, for such a decision to be carried out a thousand miles away—in Palestine, for instance. This would mean Caesar Augustus could have issued his decree, that all the world should be enrolled, several months or more prior to the angel Gabriel's visit to Mary in Nazareth. If this is true, then the Christmas story does indeed begin in Rome! The journey to Christmas starts with God's acting through worldly, political events for the purpose of allowing Jesus to be born in a manger in Bethlehem. What happened in Bethlehem started in Rome.

What does it mean for you to begin your journey to Christmas in Rome? Where do you see evidence of God's work in the world being like the rain and where do you see it like evaporation? Where can you see God clearly moving? And where do you not see God moving but choose to believe that in those places there are vapors of God's presence?

These two questions mark the difference between faith and conviction. When we see signs of God's activity and say that those signs give us faith, they don't really. What they give us is conviction, something that confirms our trust in God. It is when we can't see God moving that faith is required. In fact, what we see may challenge our faith. We may wonder why God has allowed such things to occur or where God is in the midst of confusion and pain in the world. That is when faith is required. That is when we choose to believe God is acting, even doing God's greatest work, so that by the time we see a result we can say with Jacob, "Surely the Lord is in this place—and I did not know it!" (Genesis 28:16)

Faith most often comes in retracing events that help us see God's activity versus blindly believing in what has yet to occur. That is not to say that the latter isn't a form of faith. Sometimes we do need to believe blindly, but more often faith is taking what we know, what we can see, and then choosing to believe that God was at work in these actions directing the choices, votes, decisions, and decrees even when they seem far removed from what God would want.

I have a friend in Indianapolis, Glenn MacDonald, who is a retired Presbyterian pastor. He writes a daily email devotion that goes to more than one hundred thousand people. In a recent reflection, he told a story about the dean of Gordon Conwell seminary in 1975, William Kerr. He was in his office praying one day when he was interrupted by a student, Mike Ford. The student asked what he was praying for. The president explained that there was a distinguished British scholar, Andrew Lincoln, they were trying to get on the faculty. The president knew this person could have great impact on many students, but the government wouldn't grant a work visa.

The student said, "I might be able to help with that." You see the student's father was Gerald Ford who had just become president of the United States. Within a short time, the red tape disappeared, and Andrew Lincoln was teaching at the seminary.[5]

A young student who came under Lincoln's influence was Tim Keller, the founding pastor of Redeemer Presbyterian Church in New York City. He was hugely inspired by this person. Just over a decade after leaving seminary, Keller started Redeemer and at his death in 2023 had started over 750 communities of faith around the world. His leadership and his writings have made huge impressions on Christians around the world, including me.

But retrace the steps of what brought Tim Keller under the influence of this professor. The Watergate Scandal in the early 1970s was a low point in American politics. The nation was divided unlike any time since the Civil War. President Nixon resigned. As a result, the person Nixon had appointed to be vice president, Gerald Ford, became president of the country. His son, who was a student in seminary at the time, just happened to come to the dean's office while he was praying.

In a time of turmoil when God seemed absent, events unfolded which God used to further God's purposes.

Groanings and Birth Pains

In Paul's Letter to the Romans, he captured the angst and anxiety many people feel about the world:

> *For the creation waits with eager longing for the revealing of the children of God, for the creation was subjected to futility, not of its own will, but by the will of the one who subjected it, in hope that the creation itself will be set free from its enslavement to decay and will obtain the freedom of the glory of the children of God.*
>
> *Romans 8:19-21*

Paul said the whole creation waits in eager longing. That is the mood of Advent. Advent is the first season in the Christian year.

We begin in waiting because we recognize that we are between the "already and the not yet." We will consider the topic of waiting more in depth in the next chapter, but for now we recognize that we live in the world as we know it, but we long for a world better than we know. We wait because we can't make a better world happen by our own willpower. We need help. We need God. Yet Paul spends a moment to capture the intensity of our longing. He uses other words: subjected, futility, enslavement, decay. Paul uses the language of bondage to articulate the feeling of longing. So much of Israel's history was spent in bondage. They were captive to the Egyptians, Babylonians, and eventually the Romans. Paul taps into the reality of people feeling like their lives are not their own.

Then Paul suddenly shifts metaphors. "We know that the whole creation has been groaning together as it suffers together the pains of labor" (Romans 8:22). The pain Paul talks about now is not associated with what keeps us from fully living, but what gives life. The intense pain a mother feels in giving birth is forgotten once the child is born. Paul encourages us to believe that God is doing something in the world that will one day cause our pain to subside and give way to new life. We don't see yet. All we know is the present pain, but we wait in eager longing. A child is on the way.

David Williamson is a gifted pastor I had the privilege of working alongside for eight years. He reflected in a sermon on the juxtaposition of Caesar's decree and Paul's reference to birth.

A decree went out from Caesar Augustus that all the world should be registered. That's what empires do—they decree. And to be honest, there's a part of me that wishes heaven would just decree. Don't we just want someone to impose some peace and bring some order and stability to the world? But heaven does not decree. No, God

Rome can be
a hard place
to have faith,
but it is also a place
to realize our
need for faith.

births. God sends a baby, a Son. A Son who would be killed by the empire under which he was born, suffering a Roman crucifixion. Why? So that something new could be birthed in our hearts? Whatever change needs to happen in our world begins with our being born again. For what does creation wait for with eager longing? "For the revealing of the children of God." Us, born again.[6]

I realize that Rome is not the easiest place to have faith. That may be the reason Luke begins the Christmas story there, because we all are affected by our Romes. If we allow it to happen, Rome can crush our spirit and belief in God. But acknowledging Rome prevents the Christmas story from being turned into a tonic, something that gives us a warm fuzzy, a sweet and tender story to assuage the real challenges of our world.

Beginning Christmas in Rome means God dominates the scene there as much as in the stable. God can do far more than motivate sleepless shepherds. God reigns over presidents and prime ministers. God rules generals and jailers. God inhabits the hallways of capitols and headquarters. No one on earth would have looked at a decree from Caesar Augustus and immediately thought, "God is up to something," but I imagine the angels in heaven were saying, "Get ready!"

Yes, Rome can be a hard place to have faith, but it is also a place to realize our need for faith.

I serve a congregation that I'm sure is like a lot of churches, pretty evenly divided politically. But both sides in my church have this in common: they each need faith. Several years ago, after a national election, half of the congregation was discouraged and in disbelief. They wondered, "How can God allow this person to be our president?" Four years later when the leader of the opposing party was elected the other half of the congregation asked the same question!

Any of us who care at all about the affairs of this world and the people who lead countries, counties, and communities, are routinely challenged to consider whether we are putting our faith in Rome or God. I have watched many a Christian sit slumped in a pew at the news of God's transforming work in the world who also comes to church high-fiving people after an election that went their way. When our faith rises and falls with political processes, we will always have a love-hate relationship with Rome. But remember, Rome as an empire ended nearly two thousand years ago. Empires come and go. It is the purpose of God that prevails. Looking for that purpose, seeking God's hand and presence, is what builds our faith. If Rome is the object of our worship, we will too often quit the journey of Christmas before we ever get to Bethlehem.

So, let's return to Bethlehem. Let me take you back to that moment on Christmas Eve with my friends sitting at a table in Nativity Square right after soldiers dragged away two youths that night.

We rose from our table to return to our dorm in Jerusalem. The atmosphere was not what we expected. A violent turn of events seemed to deaden our spirit. The realities of political tensions and police policies just didn't square with the serene, tender experience of Christmas we were looking for.

As we made our way to the security checkpoint, one of the guys in our group said, "Wait. What about Ahmad?" Someone responded, "What about him?" "He told us to come by, remember? He offered us chicken and rice. Let's see if he meant it."

We looked at each other as if to say, "Well, we're here. Might as well."

So we left the lights and noise of Nativity Square and headed into the back alleys of Bethlehem to find Ahmad's shop. There were no streetlights. It was after hours so no shops were open. Finally, we located his store, but it was dark inside. We knocked on the door several times but no answer. We chuckled and agreed it was all a ploy, but we were obviously too late. We began walking away, when a light inside the shop appeared. We could hear the door unlocking and opening. Ahmad peered out to see who was there. When he recognized us, he asked, "Where have you been? I gave up looking for you."

He summoned us to come inside and led us into a back room and pulled little stools into a circle, motioning for us to sit. He disappeared for a moment and returned with a massive pot of chicken and rice and sat it in the middle of the circle. He handed each of us a spoon. We stared at one another somewhat uncertain as to what to do next. He said, "Please, eat." Following his lead we all started digging spoons into this common pot. I'm sure that wouldn't meet Covid protocols today, but it was quite good. We chatted as we ate. Ahmad told us about his family, where he came from, and how he came to be in Bethlehem. He asked about our homes and families.

After we finished, he took the dish away and we whispered to each other, "Now we really have to buy something." So we stepped back into the store where wood carvings lined the shelves. He came out and asked what we were doing. We said we wanted to buy some souvenirs. With a serious and disappointed look, he said, "Please, my friends, not tonight. This is Christmas Eve. Come back in a couple days and we can do business. This is the night of our Savior's birth. Let's honor it."

When we left the shop and walked back into the dark alley, I was trying to make sense of everything I experienced that night. Whatever sense I struggled to make out of our earlier experience, I knew that this last one was special, even sacred. In a place that didn't feel all that holy, I was surprised by what became a very holy experience. Suddenly the thought occurred to me that somewhere very close to where I was standing was where Jesus was born. That night in Bethlehem was probably not all that different from the night Mary gave birth to Jesus. Bethlehem would have been crowded. So many strangers gathered in one place with a military presence would have created an air of tension. Bethlehem would not have felt like a place to feel close to God. Yet in that seemingly unholy atmosphere, Christ was born.

We will return to Bethlehem later, but I share the story of my experience that night because it symbolized the longings generated by the Romes of our world. We long for peace, unity, greater compassion among people, and an end to violence and division. I have held on to what happened that night and have come to see it as a gift, something God gave me to remember for all of my ministry ahead, for the rest of my life even, that Christ meets us in the midst of chaos and fear. He meets us in the places where we feel helpless to know how to help others. He meets when we get so weary of the world the way it is that we just want to crawl in bed and pull a pillow over our head. He meets us in our deep longings, but not always in conspicuous ways. We have to go looking. We have to seek, even if we aren't expecting to find. Because then we open ourselves to the possibility of God showing up and telling us, "I am here. I am working. There is reason to hope."

Without Rome it is unlikely that Jesus would have been born in Bethlehem. God is still in charge, even of our Romes.

CHAPTER 2

JERUSALEM

A Place of Waiting

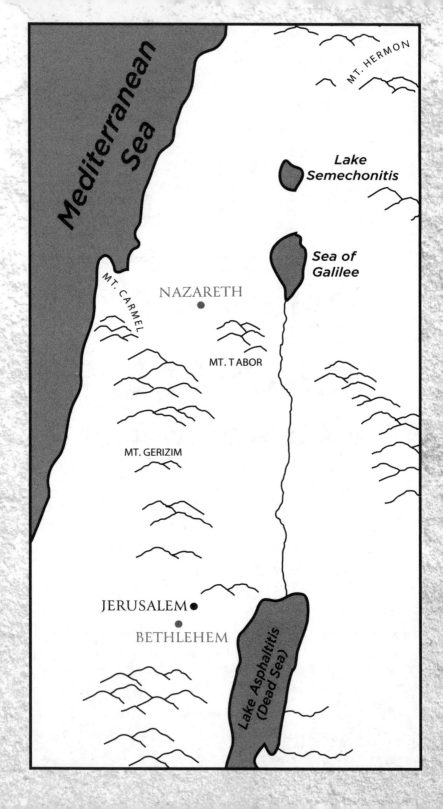

Introduction to Jerusalem

Known as the "city of peace," Jerusalem is one of the oldest cities in the world, with a population of one million residents made up of 60 percent Jews and 40 percent Palestinians. The city is sacred to the world's largest monotheistic faiths: Judaism, Christianity, and Islam. Jerusalem is located in the rocky hill country of the Judean Mountains at 2,500 feet above sea level and situated just thirty miles west of the Mediterranean Sea and twenty miles east of the Dead Sea, which sits more than 1,300 feet below sea level.

While it is hard to determine when Jerusalem was founded, references to early settlements of Jerusalem go back as far as the time of Abraham. Many believe Abraham's encounter with Melchizedek, the "priest of Salem," as mentioned in Genesis 14, is a reference to an early settlement of Jerusalem. *Shalhem* was most likely the original name of the city, taken from a Canaanite deity. This is also the root of the Hebrew word for peace, *shalom*. Also, the location where Abraham was called by God to sacrifice his son Isaac was Mount Moriah, the site of what became the Temple in Jerusalem.

The Jebusites, an ancient Canaanite tribe, are referenced in Judges 19:11 as inhabiting the city of Jebus which became Jerusalem. David conquered Jebus by sending soldiers through the water shaft of the spring of Gihon. This spring most likely explains Jerusalem's location. Producing over four hundred thousand gallons of water a day, this spring could support large numbers of people. The mount upon which the city was located was known as Zion. Once David controlled the city, he extended its border across the terraces surrounding the spring creating the City of David. On the plateau above the city, over Mount Moriah, David's son Solomon built the first Temple. The gradual expansion of residences and buildings surrounding the Temple established what is the modern location of Jerusalem. The name Zion gradually morphed into a reference to all of Jerusalem and eventually Israel itself and the world to come.

Following Jerusalem's destruction by the Babylonians in 586 BC, Jerusalem was slowly rebuilt along with the Temple. After surviving the tumultuous years following the reign of Alexander the Great, Jerusalem, and all of Israel, enjoyed a hundred years of self-governance until the takeover by Romans under General Pompey in 63 BC. This led to the appearance, culture, and lifestyle of the Jerusalem that Jesus would know. Herod the Great, early in his reign, constructed a building called the Antonia Fortress along the northwestern corner of the Temple Mount. By housing Roman soldiers in this building, it became controversial given its proximity and actual adjoining to the Temple. This is probably the location of the praetorium where the Roman governor, Pontius Pilate, tried Jesus before his crucifixion.

More than thirty years prior to that moment, was another one that continued the events leading to Jesus's birth. While synagogue worship had become a central feature of Jewish life in the centuries leading up to the time of Jesus, the Temple sacrificial system was still a dominant feature of religious life. This is what brings us to the Temple where a priest named Zechariah is serving on duty.

CHAPTER 2
JERUSALEM
A Place of Waiting

In the days of King Herod of Judea, there was a priest named Zechariah, who belonged to the priestly order of Abijah. His wife was descended from the daughters of Aaron, and her name was Elizabeth. Both of them were righteous before God, living blamelessly according to all the commandments and regulations of the Lord. But they had no children because Elizabeth was barren, and both were getting on in years.

Once when he was serving as priest before God during his section's turn of duty, he was chosen by lot, according to the custom of the priesthood, to enter the sanctuary of the Lord to offer incense. Now at the time of the incense offering, the whole assembly of the people was praying outside. Then there appeared to him an angel of the Lord, standing at the right side of the altar of incense. When Zechariah saw him, he was terrified, and fear overwhelmed him. But the angel said to him, "Do not be afraid, Zechariah, for your prayer has been heard. Your wife Elizabeth will bear you a son, and you will name him John. You will have joy and gladness, and many will rejoice at his birth, for he will be great in the sight of the Lord. He must never drink wine or strong drink; even before his birth he will be filled with the Holy Spirit. He will turn many of the people of Israel to the Lord their God. With the

spirit and power of Elijah he will go before him, to turn the hearts
of parents to their children and the disobedient to the wisdom of the
righteous, to make ready a people prepared for the Lord."

Luke 1:5-17

Our way to Christmas continues as we travel over 1,400 miles from Rome to the city of Jerusalem. In the last chapter, I shared a unique experience I had in Bethlehem, so I'll begin this chapter telling about a very unique day I had in Jerusalem. In fact, I'd call it a once-in-a-lifetime kind of day. I was filming a small-group video companion for my first book, *The God We Can Know*, based on the "I Am" sayings of Jesus. We worked with a local Israeli film crew that produced programs like the Israeli version of *Survivor*. The last day of filming was in Jerusalem, and we had a lot of ground to cover.

We started at dawn at the Tower of David, also known as the citadel, which dates back to the Crusader period and early Ottoman Empire. From there we headed to the Church of the Holy Sepulcher, the sacred church built over the site known in the Bible as Golgotha, the place where Jesus was crucified. The church also houses a tomb where it is believed that Jesus's body was laid. Our aim was to get there right as the church opened to avoid the large crowds. It was a good try!

Next, we went to the site that commemorates the Upper Room. Two important events happened here. This is where Jesus shared the Last Supper with the disciples. This is also the place where the disciples gathered after Jesus's Ascension on the Day of Pentecost as told in Acts 2. The Holy Spirit came upon them, and they began speaking ecstatically in foreign languages and talking about God's mighty acts.

Christian tour groups that visit this location usually celebrate one or the other. When we arrived, a few groups were quietly sharing

Holy Communion, so we were able to start recording. Soon another group of Pentecostal Christians began to pray and sing, getting louder as they did. The film crew finally had to set down their cameras as we realized we couldn't keep recording. They watched with wonder as members of this group began falling on the floor shouting and praying out loud. One member of the crew looked at me and asked if all American churches worship like this. I jokingly said, "I can't speak for all churches, but in my congregation, we do this just on the first and third Sundays of the month!"

Once we completed filming at the Upper Room, we headed to the Lions' Gate, now very behind schedule. The Lion's Gate was originally known as the Sheep's Gate. This gate enters the Muslim Quarter and it happened to be midday on Friday. This is the busiest moment of the week at the Lions' Gate as Muslims arrive for Friday midday prayers at the Al-Aqsa mosque or the Dome of the Rock. Cars literally scraped against each other trying to drive through the entrance. People began shouting in Arabic at one another. The film crew was unfazed by all this and decided to take a quick lunch break as we waited for the mayhem to clear.

Once we finished recording, we went to the Western Wall. An added piece of information critical to this stop is that this was during the Jewish festival of Sukkot, or "booths." In the Old Testament this is known as the Festival of Tabernacles, one of the three pilgrimage festivals. Today, Sukkot is a festive time when many Jews come to Jerusalem. It is a fun time of celebration…unless you are trying to film a resource at the Western Wall!

Loud noise and crowds didn't work well for our film crew. Plus, I didn't have a teleprompter, and I was required to memorize each recording segment. I was starting to get tired, and all of the distractions weren't making it easier. Each interruption or blunder on my part meant we had to record again.

By the time we were ready for our final stop, it was getting late in the day. We wanted a location where I could be filmed with the Dome of the Rock and the Western Wall behind me. This was not something easily found, as we would soon realize. We walked throughout a part of the old city we hoped would provide this vantage point, but no luck. Going down one street we passed a couple soldiers, both holding assault weapons. Going around the corner, the leader of the film crew jumped over a fence and climbed on a roof. A moment later he came back and said, "This is perfect. We'll film here." I said, "But what about the soldiers?" He said, "We'll shoot quickly." I thought, "And they probably will too!"

Not only did I have to do this recording wondering if soldiers were about to round the corner, but it was just minutes before the sun set on us, and I was standing at a ledge with no rail above a two-hundred-foot drop! Needless to say, I was mildly distracted. But we completed everything, and when I got back to my hotel room I paused and thought, did I really have all of those experiences in one day? Did I really get to stand in each of those locations and reflect on the biblical events that occurred there? I was overcome with the feeling of having a once-in-a-lifetime experience. Of course, I wasn't the first person that happened to in Jerusalem.

Centuries before, another religious leader had a once-in-a-lifetime experience while going about his duty at the Temple, only his came with an added surprise!

In this chapter, we arrive at the Temple in Jerusalem where we meet an elderly priest named Zechariah. His priestly division was on duty at the Temple, and Zechariah had been chosen to go into the

Holy Place and carry out the priestly functions and give a blessing to the people. To appreciate why this was a once-in-a-lifetime experience and why Luke chose to begin the story of Jesus's birth here, we need to understand the history of the Temple, the importance of Jerusalem, and what happened on this day that would play such an important role in the larger narrative of God's salvation story.

Jerusalem and Its Temple

To understand the importance of the Temple is to tell the story of Jerusalem. The Temple was built over a bit of real estate which some would say is the most significant in the world. Today, the impressive gold-overlaid Dome of the Rock, the iconic centerpiece of modern pictures of Jerusalem, sits over what is known as the Foundation Stone. In AD 621 the prophet Mohammed had a night vision in which he was transported to this location, the Temple Mount in Jerusalem. This is how the site of Judaism's holy Temple became a sacred Muslim site.

Many centuries before Mohammed's vision, this rock was known as Mount Moriah, the location described in Genesis 22 where Abraham prepared to sacrifice his son Isaac, but was stopped by an angel. Roughly eight hundred years later, King David sought to build a home for the Ark of the Covenant. David purchased Mount Moriah, known at the time as "the threshing floor of Arunah the Jebusite," as described in 2 Samuel 24. The Mount Moriah stone apparently made a suitable location for threshing wheat. As a result of purchasing this ground, David's son, Solomon, built the first Temple on this location. Scholars who have studied images of the Foundation Stone say there is an outline in the rock that fits the dimensions of the original Ark of the Covenant described in Exodus 25:10. If this is correct, that means the Holy of Holies within the Temple was constructed on the Foundation Stone.

Following the destruction of the Temple by the Babylonians in 586 BC, a second Temple was rebuilt by Zerubbabel and completed in 515. Apparently this second Temple was not as impressive as the one Solomon built. The Bible says that when this Temple was dedicated, the sound of people celebrating could not be distinguished from those who cried in disappointment (Ezra 3:12-13).

Many centuries later, when King Herod was appointed to rule over Judea, he sought to impress Rome, as well as win approval with his Jewish subjects, by rebuilding the Temple. Herod increased the footprint of the Temple Mount from Solomon's original Temple to a size roughly equal to twenty-four football fields![1] The foundation blocks Herod used were so massive that modern architects marvel over the ability of ancient builders to move and position such stones. Some say it was the largest sacred site in the Roman Empire at the time.

Even though the original Temple location is no longer under Jewish control today, it remains a holy site. The Western Wall is the nearest point to the original Temple Mount. Upon entering this area visitors pass a sign declaring that this is the closest access for Jews to the site of the Divine Presence. This real estate is revered as a place where God dwells.

As Fred Craddock recognized, "Jerusalem is the vital center; the continuity of Jesus with Judaism begins here and continues through the Gospel."[2] The story of Jesus's birth started at the Temple, but not with a pregnant mother. Rather, it began with an elderly priest and his wife.

A Chance Encounter?

The story opens by introducing us to Zechariah, a priest in the order of Abijah. This means that he was a descendant of Aaron, brother of Moses and first High Priest. There were twenty-four divisions of priests in keeping with the twenty-four grandsons of Aaron. The upkeep of the altars and performance of ritual sacrifices were assigned to these priestly divisions. Because all divisions would serve during the four festival weeks that meant each division served two different weeks to cover the rest of the year. The division of Abijah was eighth in line according to his birth order (1 Chronicles 24:10).

When a division was on duty, one priest among their number was selected by lot to go into the Holy Place, the room next to the Most Holy Place where the Ark of the Covenant was kept. The Holy Place contained three important items. First, to the right, was the Bread of Presence, which held two stacks of unleavened bread loaves, six in each, representing the twelve tribes of Israel. Each tribe was responsible for preparing their loaf that was replaced each Sabbath by the priest serving on duty. The Bread of Presence had two special meanings. First, it signified that God was their provider. The bread was symbolic of the manna in the wilderness that fed people each day to sustain them and helped them survive that difficult period. The other meaning was fellowship. A meal symbolized genuine fellowship between people. The Bread of Presence symbolized God's desire to have close fellowship and communion with God's people.

On the other side of the room was a menorah, a lampstand of pure gold with seven candles that contained olive oil that burned perpetually symbolizing God's constant presence among his people. It is said that this lampstand weighed more than 125 pounds. When Titus, the Roman general, conquered Jerusalem in AD 70 and destroyed the Temple, many of the items from the sanctuary were carried away. On a relief in Rome, known as the Arch of Titus, you can clearly see the menorah among the items carried from the Temple.

Between the Table of the Bread of Presence and the Lampstand was the Altar of Incense. The priest on duty cleaned out the ashes from this altar and replaced the incense that symbolized the prayers of the people going up to God. As it says in Revelation 5:8, the "golden bowls full of incense, which are the prayers of the saints." After the priest made the offering of incense, he said the daily prayer. Then he pressed the incense bowl into the coals, completed his work, and came out to the courtyard where people were gathered to receive a blessing from him. This occurred twice daily, once in the morning before the sacrifice was made in the outer courtyard and again at 3 p.m. when the crowds were typically larger.

Once a priest had been selected to carry out these duties, his name was removed from the list so as to give others a chance to serve. To make the offering of incense was the highest point in the life of a priest. It was truly a once-in-a-lifetime opportunity, but not every priest got to have this responsibility.

It is estimated that there were twenty thousand priests in Israel during this time. If evenly divided, there would have been more than eight hundred priests in each division. Only fourteen priests from a division were chosen for this honor each year, so roughly every ten years 140 names of priests were removed from the selection process. At any one time, about three-fourths of the members of a division were eligible to be chosen. That meant a priest had a one-in-six-hundred chance of having his name drawn by lot (and it was probably less than that). A priest would be hugely lucky to get this once-in-a-lifetime opportunity, and most never did!

Feeling Barren

We learn at the opening of this story that Zechariah had been chosen for this special duty. We also learn that his wife, Elizabeth, was also a descendant of Aaron, and they both were righteous people who had been faithful in keeping God's commandments. The honor of serving as priest in the Temple could not have gone to a more deserving person than Zechariah, a sentiment that stands out even more when we learn one last fact about Zechariah and Elizabeth. They were old and barren.

Pause.

Let that last word sink in. Barren. Not just without children. They were barren. It's a harsh word. They were not just DINKS—Double Income No Kids. They were barren. This was more than a physical description. It was an emotional and even spiritual one. Zechariah and Elizabeth were not able to participate in the covenant responsibility of having a family and producing another generation of chosen people. Not being able to have a child felt like God withheld this blessing from you. If you weren't sure why, you could assume your neighbors and relatives had their guesses.

The way to Christmas continues to the Temple in Jerusalem where an elderly couple is having a once-in-a-lifetime experience. Outwardly they presented the joy and excitement this day held, but inwardly they carried a deep hope, even if they had long since given up on that hope.

Have you ever felt barren? Have you ever waited on God to provide a breakthrough in your life but after months or years or decades, you eventually gave up belief that your prayer would be answered? What hopes do you carry within you? What are you waiting on God to do in your life or the lives of others you love or in our world?

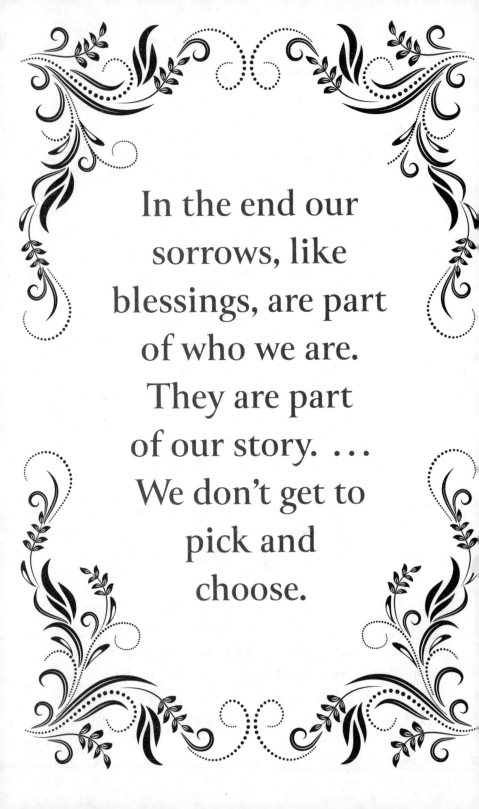

In the end our
sorrows, like
blessings, are part
of who we are.
They are part
of our story. …
We don't get to
pick and
choose.

There's an old Hasidic parable called the Sorrow Tree. It goes like this: on Judgment Day we will all be invited to hang our sorrows on a tree, and then go around the tree and choose someone's sorrows we would rather have. In other words, one day we'll get to trade our sorrows. According to the parable, we all end up choosing our own sorrows in the end.

It's easy to size people up from a distance and think, "I'd like to have their blessing," until you learn that their sorrow comes with it. You can't have one without the other. You can't go through life playing it like the stock market, buying when the times are good and selling when they are not. The blessings and the sorrows are intertwined. In the end our sorrows, like blessings, are part of who we are. They are part of our story. An unwanted part, to be sure, but who can say every part of life is wanted? We don't get to pick and choose. Being able to say that life is a blessing isn't dependent on every piece falling into place.

To arrive at Christmas, we have to contend with delays. We face stops that might feel unscheduled but in truth they are part of the journey. Waiting *is* the way to Christmas.

This is what makes Jerusalem different from Rome. Rome puts us in touch with our longings. Rome represents the things of this world we know are out of line with the way God wants the world to be. The same can apply to our individual lives. The "ought " and the "is" are often far apart both personally and globally. Longing means naming what it is we desire. But once we do, we go to Jerusalem where we hang up that longing and wait.

Jerusalem is a stop of indefinite length. You don't know how long you will be there; you just know it will be longer than you like. You walk through one of the gates of the city wall where the road leads into narrow streets lined with shops and vendors. You make your way through the store owners' shouting to get your attention until you come to an opening. Looking up, you see the magnificent Temple in the distance. Standing about fifteen stories tall with its white-washed stones, the sun's reflection makes you shield your eyes. You walk toward its long, massive walls supporting the courtyard that surrounds the Temple above and begin climbing stairs that eventually lead into the Courtyard of Gentiles. This is the widest space surrounding the Temple complex that measures about thirty-five acres! Gentiles who desired to pray to the God of Israel were allowed here.

You keep moving toward an interior wall through a large doorway known as the Beautiful Gate leading into the Courtyard of Women. This was the nearest point in which Jewish women could approach the Temple. At the opposite side of this courtyard is the entrance into a smaller area known as the Court of Israelites. This was as far as ordinary Jewish men could get to the Temple. The next area beyond this is the Court of Priests where the entrance into the sanctuary is located.

There is a small crowd gathered between the Court of Women and the Court of Israelites. They are waiting for the priest on duty to appear after conducting his ritual to give them a blessing. Among them is Elizabeth. The waiting seems unusually prolonged. They have no idea why. They will soon discover that while Zechariah was having a once-in-a-lifetime experience, he had an added surprise.

An Unexpected Moment

While Zechariah was performing his duty, an angel of the Lord appeared to him.

The story mentions that the angel was "standing on the right side of the altar of incense" (Luke 1:11) What is the significance of this detail? If Zechariah were facing the altar, then the angel stood between the altar and the table of the Bread of Presence. This bread symbolized God's provision and desire to be in fellowship with God's people. Also, the mention of the "right side" is significant. The right hand of God is often used in association with blessing and favor, as mentioned in Psalm 20:6 and 89:13. In Jesus's parable of the Sheep and Goats, the blessed are put on the right side. Could this logistical detail be Luke's way of hinting that God has come to bring blessing and favor to Zechariah?

That question will be quickly answered, but first the angel calms Zechariah's fears. Who wouldn't be afraid, standing alone in a sanctuary and suddenly being met by a celestial figure? There is a mildly humorous element to this scene. Zechariah is standing as close as he will ever get to the place of the Divine Presence. Physically he is as near to God as he'll ever be in his life. Yet the possibility of God actually showing up in that place is frightening. Is it possible to carry out religious rituals and lose any expectation of experiencing God? Keeping our hearts open to hope can be more uncomfortable than what caused us to lose hope in the first place.

If Zechariah had lost hope, then the angel was about to apply a defibrillator to his spiritual heart: "Do not be afraid, Zechariah, for your prayer has been heard" (Luke 1:13). At a time in life when he was about to start taking a pension, Zechariah learns he will have to start changing diapers. Have you ever been far enough removed from a hope that you didn't even realize you stopped hoping? We can't say for sure that was the case with Zechariah, but we can say he was shocked by this announcement.

The angel gave Zechariah a lot to chew on with the news that his wife, Elizabeth, will have a son. First, he learned that his name will be John, which means "God is gracious." Second, John will be a source of joy for his parents and many others. He will also be great in the sight of the Lord and will never drink wine or strong drink. This meant he was to be brought up in a nazirite vow (Numbers 6), meaning he is to be set apart for God. As well, he will be filled with the Holy Spirit even before his birth. (This alludes to what happened six months later when Mary, carrying Jesus inside her, came to see her relative, Elizabeth. When Mary greeted Elizabeth, John leaped inside Elizabeth's womb, and she was filled with the Holy Spirit.) Finally, the angel talking to Zechariah associated John with the prophet Elijah announcing that John will prepare people for the Lord's coming.

The angel's news was too much for Zechariah. He asked how such a thing could happen when he and his wife were so old. Shock has a way of making us forgetful. Zechariah didn't recall how God gave the same promise to Abraham and Sarah, Jacob and Rachel, and Hannah and Elkanah.

This is when Zechariah learned the angel's name: "I am Gabriel. I stand in the presence of God, and I have been sent to speak to you and to bring you this good news" (Luke 1:19). The last mention of Gabriel in the Old Testament was in the Book of Daniel. Gabriel came to interpret Daniel's vision and announce God's plans to him. We must assume Gabriel has come to do the same with Zechariah who now has this historical reality to put alongside his present uncertainty.

Gabriel, though, didn't ask Zechariah, "Do you believe me now?" Instead, he declared, "Because you did not believe my words, which will be fulfilled in their time, you will become mute, unable to speak, until the day these things occur" (Luke 1:20).

A Muted Blessing?

For a long time, this seemed to be an unfair part of the story to me. Who could blame Zechariah for asking, "How can I know?" It wasn't like God had been spectacularly present for the past four hundred years. Plus, Zechariah and Elizabeth had lived with a deep longing in their hearts without a sign or hint of answered prayer on the way. I often see myself in Zechariah. I hope. I have faith. I believe God is able to do anything. I am a pastor after all. These are helpful things to believe in my career.

But I also know, if I'm honest, what it's like to lose hope. Not lose faith. Just lose expectation that God is going to show up, change things, work a miracle, or transform some painful mess of a reality. I know what it is like to keep doing religious duty but lose a sense of anticipation that a revelation will occur in my midst. My temptation in such times is to fall on my strengths, or at least fall on my ability to do what I can. Make sure the bulletin is right, that the baptism bowl has water in it, that whatever criticisms congregants have shared are being followed up. Such doubling down on my strengths can make me critical of others I perceive are not doing the same. I think, "Just work harder like me!" What I lose in such self-reliance is the fact that God's ability to work and move is not swayed in the least by my strengths.

I recently had a good reminder of this truth. A wave of extremely cold air had come across Indiana one weekend. Upon arriving at the church that Sunday morning I learned that the heat in our chapel was not working. The temperature in the room had already dropped into the forties. Our two contemporary worship services are held in this space, the first at the same time as our traditional service in the sanctuary. I record the sermon on Fridays so it can be shown in the chapel at that hour. Calls were made and technicians were dispatched.

That Sunday was the weekend of the Martin Luther King Jr. holiday. I ended the sermon by telling the story of Claudette Colvin. We had planned to end the contemporary service by singing "This Little Light of Mine." This is usually considered to be a children's song, but it actually originated as a civil rights song. Our contemporary worship leader was going to have a soloist come down the aisle singing it very softly at the end of the sermon and then have all the praise team join her. In the traditional service, we planned to sing a hymn.

Well, everything seemed to be falling apart. Right before starting our traditional service, I learned the technicians were not going to be able to repair the furnace in time to hold services that morning, so people in the chapel were guided to the sanctuary. A few other miscues seemed to keep us from getting a flow to the service. Then, shortly before the sermon, the organist, who was having to direct the choir that morning as well, came over to me and said, "The praise team is going to do the closing song in here with our choir." My immediate reaction was to say, "No! That hasn't been rehearsed. I don't want a flop. Things have been stressful enough already." He could read my mind. He just winked at me and turned around.

I had a bit of trepidation going into the sermon, but I was relieved by the thought that it was a low attendance Sunday and therefore a failure wouldn't be as bad as it might be on other Sundays. Talk about high hopes! I finished the sermon, and the worship leader and organist began playing as the soloist walked down the center aisle of the sanctuary singing in a soulful way, "This little light of mine." We used original lyrics from the civil rights version. When the soloist reached the chancel, other vocalists joined her. The organ and piano, and even the drums, started joining in. The choir rose and began singing out with them.

What happened was nothing less than a work of the Holy Spirit. I noticed some attenders stick around for the 11 a.m. service just to experience the closing song again. Many who were there that Sunday said it was one of the most powerful endings to a service they could remember.

I know I won't forget it, and not because of the quality of the music. I get to experience that every Sunday. I'll remember that moment because it was like Zechariah was shouting in my ears. Not Zechariah the father of John the Baptist, but Zechariah the Old Testament prophet who declared, "Not by might, nor by power, but my Spirit says the Lord!" (Zechariah 4:6) When I was powerless to control what happened, God took over.

In the course of doing my religious ritual, I felt a breakthrough of God. Maybe this is why Zechariah needed to be silent while he waited through Elizabeth's pregnancy. His focus couldn't be on his activity. A priest who says prayers and blesses people depends on having a voice! If Zechariah ever did return to such duties again, he would have most likely said the same prayers and performed the same rituals, but I am sure it would have been with a much deeper conviction. Spending a season listening to the voice of God will do that.

Do you desire to hear from God? Do you feel like it has been a long time since you have, since you've had an experience of God's nearness and presence? Have you given up hearing from God and find it easier to go along doing what you have always done? Has faith become a matter of going through the motions?

If so, this may be a good season to practice silence. How might you incorporate silence, or greater amounts of listening to God, into your life right now? You could pick a time early in the morning to sit and be still before God, asking God to help you sense God's presence with you and speak to you. I personally find reading a Scripture passage before that quiet time very helpful. It centers my thoughts as I ask God, "What do you want to say to me through these words?" Perhaps another time of day will work better. Whenever it is, I recommend turning off the cell phone and getting away from distractions and interruptions. Maybe you have an area where you can walk. Nature certainly feeds my soul. Perhaps there is a wooded area near you, or a nice park where you can walk or hike and seek God's presence through the sky and trees and birds.

One of the lessons we can take away from Jerusalem is the importance of waiting. This stop on the way to Christmas challenges us to think about what we do with our longings. Waiting is not easy to do but it is a spiritual activity. You can't read the Bible closely without noticing the amount of waiting people do. The Israelites waited four hundred years to be liberated from Egyptian bondage. Abraham and Sarah waited for God's promise of a son to come true. Joseph waited through years of servitude and imprisonment before becoming the prince of Egypt. The children of Israel waited forty years, an entire generation, to enter the Promised Land. Simeon and Anna waited at the Temple their whole lives to see God's sign of salvation, and one day they were able to hold a child named Jesus. After his Ascension, Jesus told his disciples to wait for the Holy Spirit. The Bible ends with the plaintive cry, "Come, Lord Jesus!" (Revelation 22:20). This echoes the theme of Advent which means "to come to." Just as we wait for the coming of Christ, the Bible ends with all the world still waiting for the ultimate fulfillment of God's plan for creation.

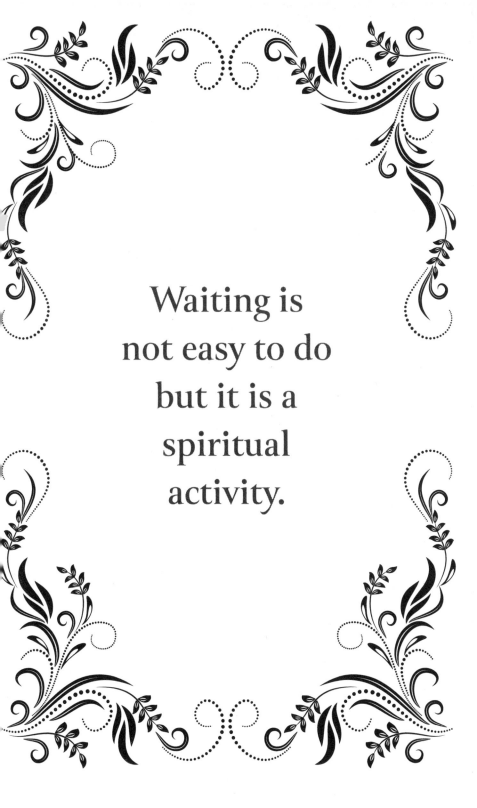

Waiting is
not easy to do
but it is a
spiritual
activity.

The Advent Invitation

Advent invites us like an old friend who calls once a year to say, "Let's get together." We show enthusiasm without commitment, but the friend is patient and unforceful. The friend invites but waits for our response. Of course, now is never a good time. Advent is always busy and seems to get busier each year. But the real reason we don't respond probably has less to do with time as it does tension. Waiting is about receiving, not getting. Waiting upon the Lord means that there are things we need that we are incapable of getting on our own, and our human nature tends toward getting. We are better getters than receivers. Get what we need. Get problems solved. Get plans made. Get a life!

Advent invites us once a year to face this tension. Waiting forces us to evaluate how well we have been able to get what we want. If we haven't succeeded, what is the reason for that? Are there things we need that come only by receiving? Receiving forces us to let go, to let go of what we want and how we want it. Waiting upon the Lord slowly opens us to what God wants and what God seeks to give.

We often think of how hard it is for us to wait on God, but have you ever wondered if it's hard for God to wait? What is the patience God shows with us? What might God be waiting for us to do? What could God be waiting to give us?

I find meaning in the fact that Zechariah's epiphany happened in the Temple. He learns that his prayer is answered and yet he still doesn't believe it. Zechariah has been going through the motions of religious life but has lost, perhaps, an expectant faith that buoys such devotion.

I find significance in all of this. I believe part of the reason Luke tells this story is to say to us, "You don't have to be certain in your faith to worship God. Your faith doesn't have to be exemplary in order for you to come before God. You can have doubts and still be accepted, because your questions, doubts, and even disbelief do not limit God's power or desire to work in your life."

Sometimes just showing up is a courageous act of faith.

I got to know a woman in our church in the early days of returning to in-person worship as Covid restrictions lessened. She responded to our call for hospitality volunteers. Because we needed to wear masks inside the building, such things as coffee service and other fellowship activities had to move outside.

This was an intense period of grief for this woman. Her husband of many years got Covid and was put in isolation in the Intensive Care Unit of the hospital. His condition worsened, but she was unable to visit him. He eventually died, and she was heartbroken not just by his death but the thought of him being alone attached to machines and tubes.

Compounding her grief was the isolation of living in an empty house cut off from community. She watched services online, and when we announced the need for volunteers, she was one of the first to call. By the time we were able to move our fellowship offerings inside again she had taken over the leadership of this ministry. She was finding joy in serving others. Her effusive smile and interactions with people left them amazed when they later discovered what had happened in her life. She didn't get answers for her loss. She never received a reason for her husband getting Covid, but she did receive peace and awareness of the presence of God.

Sometimes God doesn't give us what we want or when we want it, but God is faithful to give us what we need when we wait and just show up.

Why Does God Take So Long?

But there is still a nagging question left to consider: Why? Why does God take so long? We're not talking about precedent. We know the examples of faith. Abraham and Sarah had to wait for a promised son. Israel prayed for deliverance for four hundred years. Even then, they had to wait another forty years to get to the Promised Land. The Old Testament ended with people waiting for a Messiah to come. The New Testament ended with people praying for Jesus to return: "Come, Lord Jesus." We know there is precedent for waiting in faith. The question is why? Why doesn't God act quicker?

The experience of Zechariah and Elizabeth may offer some insight. Notice that Zechariah and Elizabeth's answer to prayer was part of a bigger story. As Gabriel said to Zechariah, "Do not be afraid, Zechariah; for your prayer has been heard. Your wife Elizabeth will bear you a son . . . He will turn many of the people of Israel to the Lord their God" (Luke 1:13,16).

There was more at stake than just fulfilling the wish of an elderly couple. The hope in Zechariah and Elizabeth's story was a part of God's story of hope. The key to finding meaning in our waiting is to ask how our longing fits into God's bigger purpose. How might God use our situation?

If you are tempted to get jealous of Zechariah and Elizabeth and think that at least their prayer was answered, then realize that their answered prayer was not just for them. Think for a moment about what happened to their son, John the Baptist. We don't know how long Zechariah and Elizabeth lived, but if they lived long enough, then they saw their son get arrested by Herod and put in prison where he was eventually beheaded. God gave Zechariah and Elizabeth a magnificent blessing, an answer to a prayer they perhaps had stopped praying. That answer, though, was not the sole possession of Zechariah and Elizabeth. John was an answer for many other people and his life was part of God's story. John was faithful to his call even to the point of death.

For Zechariah and Elizabeth there was pain either way. There was not only the pain of long waiting but also the pain of receiving and having to let go. At least in the case of the latter, they were able to let go knowing how their son had been used by God and how his life was a blessing to many others. Perhaps John's own faithfulness was a product of what happened to Zechariah and Elizabeth in their waiting. As they trusted God, in spite of years of not receiving, they developed a dependence on God so that when the answer finally came, they understood this gift was about more than the two of them.

One of the best answers I have ever found for why God makes us wait comes from something I read many years ago by John Ortberg. He said, "What happens in us while we wait is as important as what we're waiting for."[3] Let that sink in for a moment. What God does in us while we wait is as important as what we wait for. That's a powerful thought. We discover the truth only when we wait in Advent fashion. Advent-style waiting is not biding time or pacing the floor. It is waiting like Zechariah. It is continuing to show up, to carry out our devotion, and to pray, "May the God of mercy come."

Notice Luke begins and ends the Gospel in Jerusalem at the Temple. Preparing for Jesus started with Zechariah in the Temple. After the Resurrection and Ascension, the waiting continued for the disciples who "were continually in the temple blessing God" (Luke 24:53). The Temple is the place where prayers are sometimes answered, but most of the time it is where people gather to wait and pray, "Come, Lord Jesus."

So, as you hurry on your way to Christmas, take time to pause and pray and make your requests known to God.

What are you waiting for?

CHAPTER 3
NAZARETH
A Place of Simplicity

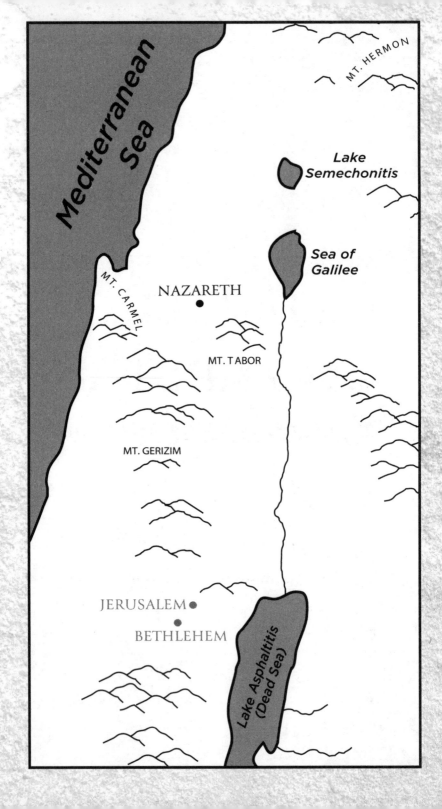

Introduction to Nazareth

The city of Nazareth is located among rolling hills roughly fifteen miles west of the Sea of Galilee. To the east, just five miles away, is Mount Tabor, the site of the Transfiguration. At 1,900 feet, Mount Tabor towers over the fertile vineyards and fields that flourish in this region. Yet in spite of its agricultural surrounding, Nazareth has become a hub for Arab-owned technology and software companies, thus earning the nickname, "the Silicon Valley of the Arab Community." The city today is nearing one hundred thousand residents, the largest in its district, and is the biggest Arab city in Israel with a 70 percent Muslim and 30 percent Christian population.

Archaeologists have found remains in the area that go back to prehistoric periods. Civilizations may have formed in this region as early as 9,000 BC. Nazareth gets its name, however, from biblical times. *Netzer* is the Hebrew word for "branch." Tradition has it that Nazareth was named for the verse in Isaiah 11:1, "A shoot shall come up from the stump of Jesse; from his roots a Branch will bear fruit" (NIV). This verse alludes to the promise of a Messiah that will come from the lineage of King David. Perhaps early Jewish inhabitants gave Nazareth this name in the hope that a Messiah would come from their village one day.

Today, Nazareth attracts Christian pilgrims who come to see and revere the place where Jesus was raised. The beautiful Church of the Annunciation is built over ruins believed to be a home dating back to the first century and honored as the home of Mary, the mother of Jesus, and the site of the angel Gabriel's annunciation to her. Just a few blocks from the church is a recreated biblical village that imagines what Nazareth would have been like at that time and gives visitors a chance to experience ancient shepherding, pottery and wine making, cooking, synagogue worship, and more. Nazareth is also the starting point of a forty-mile path called The Jesus Trail that winds toward Galilee through many of the towns and locations of Jesus's ministry.

When Jesus was a boy, Nazareth would have been incredibly small even for that time. Estimates by historians range from one hundred to four hundred people. Josephus, a Roman-Jewish historian of the first century, doesn't even mention Nazareth among the forty-five towns of the Galilee district. Figuratively speaking, Nazareth would have sat in the shadow of a much larger and more notable city called Sepphoris located just a few miles away. While Sepphoris wasn't very large through much of its history, Herod Antipas, son of Herod the Great, invested heavily in building it into an impressive city. Jesus would have grown up watching the construction and development of Sepphoris and no doubt this would have brought work to his father, Joseph, who was a carpenter.

The reason Nazareth was not given this attention may be for the fact that it was not located near a major water source or highway. A well provided its only drinking water, thus limiting the number of people who could live there. Today this well is commemorated as the Well of Mary and it is here, one tradition says, that Mary was standing when she was visited by the angel Gabriel. While going about daily chores, she had a heavenly encounter. That encounter is what brings us to Nazareth.

CHAPTER 3
NAZARETH
A Place of Simplicity

In the sixth month the angel Gabriel was sent by God to a town in Galilee called Nazareth, to a virgin engaged to a man whose name was Joseph, of the house of David. The virgin's name was Mary. And he came to her and said, "Greetings, favored one! The Lord is with you." But she was much perplexed by his words and pondered what sort of greeting this might be. The angel said to her, "Do not be afraid, Mary, for you have found favor with God. And now, you will conceive in your womb and bear a son, and you will name him Jesus. He will be great and will be called the Son of the Most High, and the Lord God will give to him the throne of his ancestor David. He will reign over the house of Jacob forever, and of his kingdom there will be no end." Mary said to the angel, "How can this be, since I am a virgin?" The angel said to her, "The Holy Spirit will come upon you, and the power of the Most High will overshadow you; therefore the child to be born will be holy; he will be called Son of God. And now, your relative Elizabeth in her old age has also conceived a son, and this is the sixth month for her who was said to be barren. For nothing will be impossible with God." Then Mary said, "Here am I, the servant of the Lord; let it be with me according to your word." Then the angel departed from her.

Luke 1:26-38

The Mississippi River is the longest in the United States. Before reaching the Gulf of Mexico at New Orleans, the river winds more than 2,300 miles through ten states. The Mississippi River spans several miles in width, and actually gets as wide as eleven miles at one point. However, at its headwaters at Lake Itasca, Minnesota, the Mississippi River is just a few feet wide. You can step across it, and even if you can't, the water is not much more than ankle deep. A river few people could swim across for much of its length can be spanned in just a few steps at its starting point. What appears insignificant in the beginning becomes the most important waterway in the country.

You can tell where this is going, right? Beginning places are not always good predictors of possibility. Think of the television show, "South Park." Okay, this is a big jump from talking about rivers, but "South Park" is a popular animated television series that has been around for twenty-seven seasons and running. Known for its edgy content and sometimes dark satirical humor, the show is based on the fictional community of South Park, Colorado. Only, it's a real place.

Recently my wife and I were in Denver visiting some longtime friends. While we were there, they took us on a hike. We got up early one morning before daylight to drive several hours to the trailhead of Mount Sherman, one of the "fourteeners" in central Colorado. On the way we came to an expansive high plateau surrounded by giant mountains in the distance. The morning sun had just started to crest over the distant peaks, and we got a full view of this massive range of green pastures. The husband, who was driving, explained that this valley was known as South Park, with the same name as the fictional town created by Trey Parker and Matt Stone.

"Get outta here!" was my response. I had a hard time believing that such a popular, salty television show could have started in a remote place like this.

"Seriously," he said, "this is where they grew up."

Only a few ranch houses could be spotted for miles, and there was not a stoplight in sight. When you want to get away from it all, you go to South Park, Colorado! This didn't square with what I knew about the show. It takes on the toughest social issues in our country in a way that probably offends everyone at some point. One would never think that the creators of a major, award-winning television program could come from such an obscure location, much less a show that takes on topics like abortion, same-sex marriage, antisemitism, censorship, violence, racism, and more. South Park seemed like the kind of place you go to escape issues like these. Instead, it gave rise to a show that takes on these problems in a no-holds-barred format.

Places of origin are not always predictors of possibility. But let's understand, especially in this example, that South Park, Colorado, is not significant because two people who grew up there went on to create a major television show. What makes South Park significant is a different question. You would have to grow up there to really know. But whatever is significant about it might be what influenced or motivated Trey Parker and Matt Stone to create a show they named after the place where they were raised.

So, where one begins isn't always an indication of where one ends up, and what appears insignificant can be significance in disguise. With that, we are ready for the next stop on the way to Christmas, a tiny village perhaps as small as South Park, Colorado...Nazareth of Galilee.

The Value of Nazareth

Today you would not use words like insignificant, tiny, or obscure to describe Nazareth. Nazareth is a bustling city. The rapid growth keeps its narrow streets congested. Honking horns, bicycles, and tourist buses are in abundance. Construction cranes tower above the dusty hills around the city as housing developments and office buildings continue to be built.

Nazareth is home to the largest Arab community in Israel with Muslims outnumbering Christians about two to one. Islamic prayers broadcast from speakers attached to minarets are heard at the fives prayer periods each day. The diversity of faces, religions, and languages is noticeable at every turn. The city itself can be somewhat disconcerting if you expect to find a quiet, slow-paced village.

Most people who visit Nazareth are Christian pilgrims traveling to see the Church of the Annunciation. To get into the courtyard surrounding the church you must wade through tourist groups who have come there from around the world. Along one side of the courtyard is a colonnade with beautiful religious artwork that represent gifts from various countries.

Stepping through the doors and walking into the church you quickly feel as if you have entered another world, which is the designed effect. Many churches built at such holy sites are meant to convey a sense of leaving the secular and entering the sacred, a sort of other-worldly experience. The Church of the Annunciation provides the feeling that the noise and bustle outside is left behind. You are now drawing near to a God-inhabited space. Of course, God inhabits all spaces, but places like this help you to be mindful of the sacred all around us. The point is to carry the sanctuary into the world and not the other way around!

The Church of the Annunciation commemorates the site where it is believed the angel Gabriel visited Mary and announced that she was to be the mother of the Savior of the world. Luke is the only Gospel to record this event: "Greetings, favored one! The Lord is with you," said the angel (Luke 1:28).

Mary is uncertain what the greeting means, but Gabriel assures her that she has no reason to be afraid. In fact, just the opposite. He says, "You have found favor with God. And now, you will conceive in your womb and bear a son, and you will name him Jesus" (Luke 1:30-31). The suddenness of the greeting and dialogue almost underplays the impact of what is taking place. God is taking on human form in this young girl.

In the Church of the Annunciation, archaeological foundations of a first-century home are exposed and visible beneath the floor of the church. Tradition has credited this as the home of Mary and her family. A cupola at the center of a dome high above the sanctuary allows light to stream below conveying a sense of God's presence coming down over the house. You get the sense that the earthly and eternal meet inside this church.

Below the sanctuary is a grotto dating back to the third or fourth century, perhaps a part of the original building commissioned by Emperor Constantine, whose mother Helena sought to build churches over important Christian sites in the Holy Land. Walking down the dark stairwell, you come to a small chapel. At one end there is an altar with a phrase engraved in Latin, "Verbum caro hic factum est." It means "The Word became flesh here."

I remember the feeling I got when I stood there for the first time and heard those words translated into English. I was no longer just taking a tour of another church at another historic location. This was the place God stepped from eternity into the limitations of time and space. Of course, you can never know with certainty that this was the exact location, but as tour leaders are fond of saying, "If it wasn't here, it was near."

This is where the Word became flesh! The translation for "word" comes from the Greek *logos*, from which we also get the word logic.

The divine *logos* conveys more than just the idea that God speaks to us. God is the logic that holds the universe together. The ancient Greek philosopher Heraclitus was one of the first people to identify this concept. He noted that the world is always changing. Nothing stays the same. At times this seems meaningless and illogical. Think of the writer of Ecclesiastes venting his frustrated search to make sense of life and constantly returning to the refrain, "Everything is meaningless!" (1:2 NIV)

Heraclitus, though, recognized that there is a sameness to the universe. The sun rises and sets each day. The stars have a pattern. The seasons come and go. In the midst of all that changes, there is a hidden logic.

John's Gospel claimed this logic in terms of faith. What holds the universe and all of life together is not a nameless philosophy, but God. "In the beginning was the Word, and the Word was with God, and the Word was God.... The Word became flesh" (John 1:1, 14). Standing deep below the surface of the ground in that dark grotto in Nazareth, I had an overwhelming sense of the holy all around me. God's divine logic, the one who holds life together, became flesh...here!

The journey to Christmas goes through Nazareth. This is where God's love became specific. At a particular time, to a particular girl, in a particular place, God chose to become flesh. Who would have thought that a place like Nazareth would be the origin of the Savior of the world?

Why Nazareth?

But why here? Why Nazareth? In that time, Nazareth was very different from its modern reality. Nazareth was a tiny, seemingly irrelevant village with a population that, from best estimates, ranged

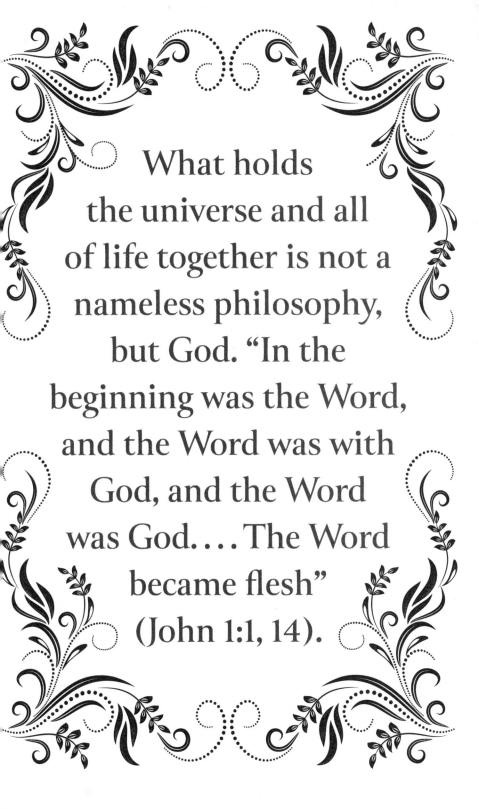

What holds the universe and all of life together is not a nameless philosophy, but God. "In the beginning was the Word, and the Word was with God, and the Word was God.... The Word became flesh" (John 1:1, 14).

from a handful of families to as many as a couple hundred people. Nazareth's size has a lot to do with its location. It was not situated on a main road or thoroughfare that would have brought regular travelers, visitors, and merchants to the village. Nazareth was also not located near a large water source like a river or reservoir. The main water supply was a single well, today called "Mary's Well," which would have provided only enough water to serve a limited number of people.

Therefore, Nazareth was virtually unknown at the time. Jewish historian, Josephus, who wrote about the Jews during the reign of Emperor Vespasian, mentions that there were 240 towns in upper and lower Galilee, but he makes no mention of Nazareth. The Hebrew Bible, the Talmud, nor the Midrash make any mention of Nazareth.

Nazareth seems to have been a disrespected place. When Jesus started his ministry and invited Philip to follow him, Philip went to Nathaniel and shared the news that he had found the one who was described by Moses and the prophets, Jesus from Nazareth. Nathaniel, perhaps with as much sarcasm as honest inquiry, replied, "Can anything good come out of Nazareth?" (John 1:46)

I live in Indianapolis. With its universities, medical centers, major corporations, and professional sports teams, no one would call Indianapolis insignificant. But before many of these developments came about over the last fifty years, Indianapolis was not nearly the busy city it is today. It didn't have the entertainment and conventions like it does now to keep the downtown so active. Back then Indianapolis was jokingly called "India-no-place."

Nazareth seems like it was a no-place to most people at the time the angel Gabriel visited Mary. Clearly it was not a place expected to produce anything or anyone of promise.

Why, then, was Nazareth a place God sent Gabriel on a recruiting mission to find a suitable mother for Jesus? What was it about Nazareth that would have shaped and influenced a young girl in such a way as to find favor with God? What spiritual meaning can we take away from a visit to Nazareth that helps us in our own journey to experience Christ and prepare for his coming among us?

A Simple Life

For one thing, consider the simplicity of a place like Nazareth. Life would have been lived at a much slower, less frenetic pace. However, I don't want to say it would have been less complicated. Life in ancient Nazareth would have had its complexities. People lived under foreign rule. The Romans had been in control for more than half a century ending the short one-hundred-year reign of self-governance for Israel—something they would not have again until 1948. There was also dependence on the weather for resources. The Galilean area can become very dry and arid during long periods of the year, often limiting the ability to grow produce and keep livestock watered and fed. Disease and injury were always a concern. Medical care for such a small village would have been limited.

What people had, though, was each other. These conditions would have raised the level of dependence people place on one another for support and survival. Families would have known each other well and no doubt helped and looked after one another. There would have been a strong sense of security and support. When life is unhurried, we have time to get to know those we live near so that we build a sense of responsibility for everyone's well-being. We become more willing to depend on others.

I have a friend who grew up in an area of Indianapolis known as Haughville. When he was a child, this was a poor community populated by various ethnic groups and nationalities. This man had grown up in a largely Slovenian neighborhood that was strongly Catholic. He says he didn't have the chance to get into trouble growing up. Every mother looked after each other's children. More than once he said a neighbor mom would grab him by the ear and say, "Tommy, I am taking you home right now to your mother!"

Maybe like Haughville, Nazareth had moms who stuck together, sort of like a parental union. Getting into trouble might not have been option growing up in Nazareth, but the significance of such a place runs deeper. Nazareth would have lacked the entertainment and conveniences of larger cities, but there would have been fewer distractions, and such simplicity has a byproduct.

The Value of Simplicity

We live in a time when access to information has become close to addictive. The need to gain more and better data becomes overwhelming and even paralyzing. Taking away options and limiting our resources can be freeing. Abraham Lincoln grew up with little to read and that may explain why he achieved the depth of thought he had. In David Donald's biography on Lincoln, he points out that Lincoln had access to the Bible, Aesop's Fables, and just a few other books. His stepmother said, "He must understand everything—even to the smallest thing—minutely and exactly. He would then repeat it over and over to himself again and again...and when it was fixed on his mind to suit him, he never lost that fact or the understanding of it."[1] Such limited resources produced a mastery of focus and deep intellect.

We all need a Nazareth where we can simplify, reduce distractions, and be free to think, contemplate, and listen. We need those places where we can listen to God, where we are open to the possibility of interruption and intrusion, where God can break in and get our attention. Perhaps your Nazareth looks like a closet in the house or a chair in the yard or a park bench or a table at the library or a pew in an empty sanctuary.

Susannah Wesley, wife of John Wesley, raised eleven children. Being responsible for the cooking, cleaning, and teaching for that size of family left little time for prayer and devotions. At the Wesley home in Epworth, England, several years ago, a tour guide explained that Susannah had a practice when she took breaks in her kitchen. She would sit down and pull her apron over her head. This gave her privacy and separation to reconnect with God and center herself. I'm sure the children learned when they walked in and saw their mom with the apron over her head, do not disturb![2]

Do you have a Nazareth where life can slow down and quiet down?

There's Significance, and Then There's Significance

Of course, while Nazareth was somewhat secluded, this doesn't mean it was cut off from the rest of the world. Just six kilometers (about three-and-a-half miles) to the west was the city of Sepphoris. Though not mentioned anywhere in Scripture, nonbiblical Jewish writings associate Sepphoris with a city dating back to the time of Joshua. Herod the Great liberated the city after it had been captured by an ancient Persian empire. Following the death of Herod, the territory of Galilee was turned over to his son, Herod Antipas, who invested heavily in rebuilding Sepphoris to a level of prestige and prosperity not previously known. It was regaled as the "jewel of Galilee," built with paved streets, public buildings, markets, bathhouses, and a theater, which was not common for Galilean towns. Sepphoris gave the appearance of Roman opulence and power. That was an important way for local leaders, especially Jewish ones like Herod Antipas, to gain the attention of Rome.

Much of this period of rebuilding Sepphoris took place during Jesus's childhood. His father, Joseph, was a carpenter. Scholars believe Joseph would have worked in Sepphoris when Jesus was a boy. Jesus probably grew up hearing his dad come home at the end of the day describing the job sites where he worked, what the people were like, the things they talked about, what he heard them say about Rome and politics and culture. Jesus would have learned much about life beyond Nazareth. He may have grown up in a no-place, but he would have probably been worldly wise.

For villages like Nazareth and the many others dotted around the Galilean region, Sepphoris would have been the "it" place to be. If you wanted to be somebody or know somebody, at least according to worldly values, then you needed to spend time in Sepphoris.

Of course, Sepphoris doesn't exist today. Aside from archaeologists who spend weeks at a time digging among the ruins, no one lives there. At one time Sepphoris was a place to feel significant, but Nazareth was, in fact, the place to find significance. One had more of a future than the other.

I recently shared in a sermon at my current church about a congregation I served during the economic recession in 2008. Many people in that community had lived a very upwardly mobile life carrying large debt and big mortgages. Suddenly faced with job layoffs and salary reductions, people were struggling to make ends meet.

One woman in the church had experienced a personal recession several years before the rest of the community. Her husband had a major health setback, forcing him to leave his job. They had to sell their dream home and move with their five children into a much smaller house. She learned ways to economize and save. Years later, when she heard other women in the church question how to save money, she started holding classes to pass along tips she had discovered. This included insights like how to maximize shopping with coupons. She discovered you can increase the value of coupons by learning which stores offer rewards like double and triple value days. She also taught ways to cook healthy, affordable meals.

Many families hardly cooked at home, and much less shopped with coupons. They were amazed by the amount of money they could save. As they discussed these practices, some would remember times when they were little when they would cut coupons out of the Sunday paper with their moms. They started creating this ritual with their own kids.

Others remembered experiences growing up when they shared meals with neighbors. One night they would prepare extra portions and carry the surplus to neighbors who in turn did the same on following nights. They began replicating this tradition in their neighborhoods. Over time people began to say things like, "I don't want to go back to the way things used to be where we ate at the country club and nitpicked whether the chicken was overcooked." Their challenges allowed them to rediscover things in life that mattered.

As I shared this story with my congregation that morning, I was surprised by the number of heads I saw nodding. People made a point to tell me after the service how they grew up doing some of the same things. Perhaps you too can recall times in your life that were simpler.

Are there rituals or routines you would like to pick up again? Have you gone through a time when it felt like things of significance in your life were stripped away? What could be a new level of significance you can find in this new place? Could simplifying life be part of the answer?

The Value of a Simple Faith

Consider again the words carved in the altar of the grotto beneath the Church of the Annunciation. The Latin phrase means "The Word became flesh here." That bit of earth is revered today. A magnificent church sits over the turf where it is believed Gabriel stood before Mary, where God became flesh. But what made that location significant? Was it the place or the person? Was it Nazareth or Mary? Was the "here" a house or a heart?

The Gospel of Luke says that Mary found favor with God. What does that mean? This statement gives the impression that there was something about Mary that was deserving of this visit by the angel. Maybe it was Mary's faith or her humility, or perhaps even her goodness. Catholic tradition holds that Mary was sinless and therefore was worthy to be the mother of Jesus. The problem with such conjectures is they are not mentioned in the Bible. There is nothing said of Mary being sinless or possessing special qualities that merited her being favored by God.

So, was there something about Mary or not?

Let's look a little closer at the word translated "favored." It is translated to mean grace: *charis*. Grace is God's gift. Grace is the gift of God's kindness, mercy, and love. We don't earn or deserve grace. This is what makes grace a gift. We simply receive grace and welcome it into our lives, which presumes, of course, an understanding or awareness that God's grace is something we need.

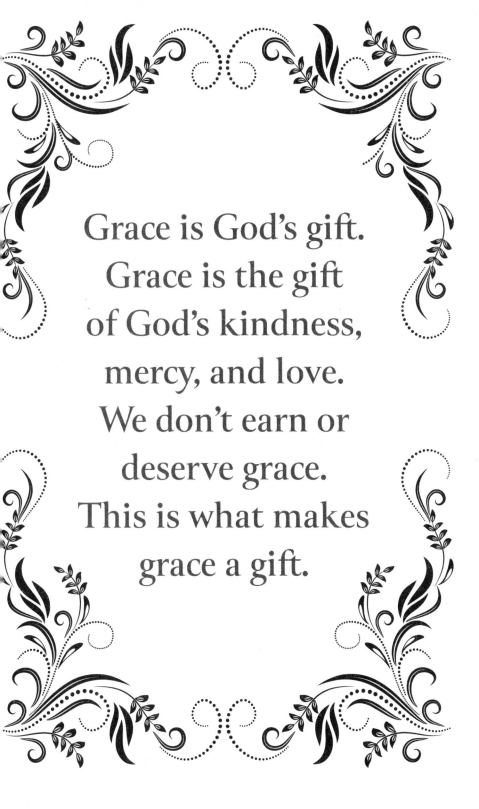

Grace is God's gift.
Grace is the gift
of God's kindness,
mercy, and love.
We don't earn or
deserve grace.
This is what makes
grace a gift.

If there is any reason God chose Mary that is associated with her character, "That reason lies tucked away in the purposes of God,"[3] as Fred Craddock wrote. What we can say for sure is that Mary cooperated with God's purpose, she opened herself to God's favor, and she willingly accepted an assignment from the Lord.

Just as Nazareth may seem a surprising choice for Gabriel to visit over, say, a place like Sepphoris, so may the choice of person seem equally surprising. The story of the Annunciation begins with the mention of the time being the sixth month. But the sixth month of what? The answer is Elizabeth's pregnancy, which is the subject of the story told in the Gospel of Luke immediately before the Annunciation. Elizabeth was the wife of Zechariah and a relative of Mary. Zechariah was a priest who had also been visited by the angel Gabriel while he was serving on duty in the Temple in Jerusalem. Gabriel announced that Zechariah and Elizabeth would have a child even though they were biologically too old to do so. The child would prepare the way for the Lord's coming.

Now, if most of us were writing this story we would have most likely reversed the assignments. Elizabeth was the wife of a respected priest. She was even a descendant of the high priest Aaron. She had legacy credentials. She was also older and wiser. If character did have anything to do with bearing the Savior of the world, then Elizabeth would certainly qualify since she was described as righteous in the sight of God, walking blamelessly in all the commandments and requirements of the Lord (Luke 1:6). If you were writing the ideal job qualifications for "Mother of the Lord," then Elizabeth checked all the boxes.

Mary, on the other hand, was very young and inexperienced. She didn't come from a priestly line. She wasn't even married, only engaged—and to a carpenter at that. She hadn't done anything up to that point in her life worth mentioning as worthy qualifications for such an assignment. But that might be the reason God chose Mary. God made her full of grace. God favored her. Who better to carry the life of Jesus within her than someone who could not brag on her ancestry, her heritage, her worth or status, or her accomplishments. Grace has nothing to do with those things. Grace is God's gift. Mary would later sing,

"My soul magnifies the Lord,
and my spirit rejoices in God my Savior,
for he has looked with favor on the lowly state of his servant.
Surely from now on all generations will call me blessed,
for the Mighty One has done great things for me,
and holy is his name;
indeed, his mercy is for those who fear him
from generation to generation."

Luke 1:46-50

Think about this for a moment. From the time of the Annunciation until Jesus's birth, wherever Mary went she carried Jesus within her. Have you ever known people who carry Jesus within them? Everywhere they go, every encounter with people, they convey grace, kindness, and love from deep within them. They don't come off as proud or haughty. What they leave with people are not impressions of their own accomplishments or authority or identity. They leave goodness. They don't need to receive value from others. They give value. It's as if everywhere they go, they leave grace.

There was something about Mary. She was willing to embody God's grace and that certainly transferred to Jesus. She welcomed the wonder and mystery and intimidation of this unique calling.

She valued not her own worthiness but the fact that God found her worthy. She was free to give grace because she was given grace.

What would it look like for you to be full of grace? Perhaps a good starting point would be to pray for God's grace to fill you and help you rely not on your own strengths but on God's favoring. What does it mean to let God be enough for us? So many of us are running on empty. We are so desperate for what we want God to do for us, it's hard to even imagine what God can do through us. But the two can be the same.

A woman in our church wrote me to say how desperate she had been for God to show up in her life. Walking through a divorce, having to change homes, trying to care for young children, she felt depleted and alone. While she had been praying for God to save her marriage, allow her to keep her home, and give her the strength to raise her children well, she got to the point of just needing to feel God's presence. That would be enough, but even that prayer didn't seem to be answered.

One day she was challenged with the idea of being the answer to prayer she sought. Be a reassuring presence, be the love, be the grace she so desperately needed. She wasn't ready to give up on her faith and walk away from God. But she also knew that her prayers weren't bringing her the breakthrough she needed, so she gave this idea a try. She started focusing on the needs of others and what she could do for them. She practiced being present with people, listening to their hurts, reassuring them, showing care for them. She would pray with people. As time and energy afforded, she would even help them in practical ways. Over time she said God didn't remove her challenges, but strangely she did feel God's presence in unexpected ways. She felt God's love for her, and those experiences gave her the courage and hope she needed.

The Value of a Simple Truth

Let me offer one last thought about Nazareth, and this observation may be so simple it seems simplistic: Nazareth was a place where God showed up. That is an obvious point to take away from the story I know, but it is most important, especially if you are in a place where others say nothing good can come from there. If you start to believe the place where you are is insignificant, you will start to feel a lack of significance about your life and what can become of it. If you start to believe nothing good can be found where you are, then goodness itself will fade from life.

Have you been to Nazareth? Do you know what it is like to be in a place that gets overlooked by others? You might have thoughts like this: "Maybe if I lived in a place where I knew more people and had more contacts, my resume would have gotten attention." "If only I was in a different school my application might have been accepted." "I suppose people just forgot where I was." "I don't feel like I can experience God in this place." If you have ever felt or said any of these statements or ones similar, then just remember, "In the sixth month, the angel Gabriel was sent by God to a town in Galilee called Nazareth" (Luke 1:26).

There is no place we can find ourselves where God will not show up. That is the lesson of Nazareth, a lesson repeated throughout Scripture. God found Joseph, son of Jacob, in a prison in Egypt. God came to Gideon while Gideon was hiding in a winepress. God met Elijah after he ran into a wilderness to end his life. God spoke to Moses on a remote desert mountain where he was living as a fugitive. The psalmists who asked, "How could we sing the Lord's song in a foreign land?" (137:4) also confidently declared, "Where can I go from your spirit? Or where can I flee from your presence? (139:7)

The Word became flesh here. Say those words to yourself right now. "Here" is right where you are. Yes, God became flesh in a specific place at a specific time in history, but through Jesus's death and resurrection God becomes real to all people in all times *in all places!* Here becomes everywhere to God.

Richard Rohr, the Catholic author and founder of The Center for Contemplation and Action in New Mexico, calls this having a truly incarnational worldview. In one of his writings, he talks about going on a hermitage to Kentucky. The hermits who lived on the grounds were especially reclusive, venturing out of their abodes on rare occasions like Holy Week and Christmas. Walking the grounds one day Rohr was excited to see one of these holy men walking toward him. He recognized the person as a former abbot, but didn't want to interrupt his reclusion, so he just stood there. The hermit knew that Rohr was on the grounds. He came up to him and said, "Richard, when you preach, be sure to tell the people, *God is not out there!* Thank you."

Reflecting on the encounter Rohr wrote: "The reclusive had a worldview I would call truly Christian: Incarnational. It is actually not too common, even among baptized Christians. The vast majority of Christians I have met worldwide are actually atheists, but not Incarnational at all. God is still out there, invited into things, and they are all inviting God to come to them...It is always a matter of getting God down here and us up there."[4]

The Incarnation means the Word became flesh *here*. God is with us right now. This makes Nazareth a most important stop on the way to Christmas. Nazareth teaches us that while the place where we are feels empty and insignificant, far removed from the place we thought life would take us, it is still a place full of God's presence. We don't have to beg and cajole God to come down. God is here. God is with us.

Sometimes the only way we endure difficult times is through the presence of God that meets us. However, just because God is in our hard places doesn't suddenly transform them into something good. Here can include hell with God. There is a line from the original Apostles' Creed we don't include in our modern versions, but many versions show the asterisk where it has been removed. Jesus "suffered under Pontius Pilate, was crucified, died, and was buried; he descended to the dead (hell). On the third day he rose again…" Even our own hells are places where Jesus is.

Well, it is time to pack up and head to the next stop on our journey, but before we go, turn around and take one last look at Nazareth. Not the modern city with busy streets and honking horns and an incredible edifice commemorating the Annunciation. Instead, try to picture the Nazareth of the first century. It was a lot like the headwaters of the Mississippi River, a place so small many people stepped over it. You might hear a few bleating sheep. There's perhaps a stream or two of smoke rising from some fires where people are cooking meals. About the time you wonder what there is to see here, you notice a girl walking to the well to draw water. Suddenly she seems startled. You can't make out why, but she appears to be talking to someone.

This is when you realize what happened in this tiny, insignificant place. What started out as a trickle became a torrent of power that forever changed history. The knowledge of God's personal love for us, the forgiveness of the cross, the deeds of mercy that have become hospitals and orphanages and schools around the world all flowed from this place. God's love is still flowing, and the river moves through us.

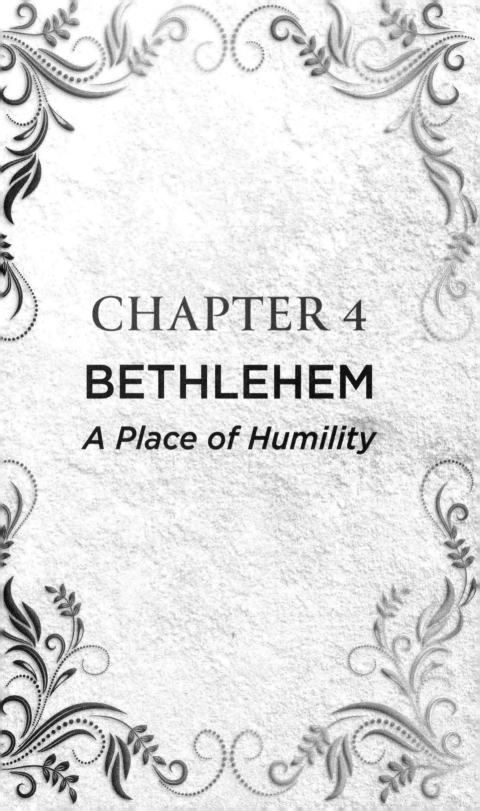

CHAPTER 4
BETHLEHEM
A Place of Humility

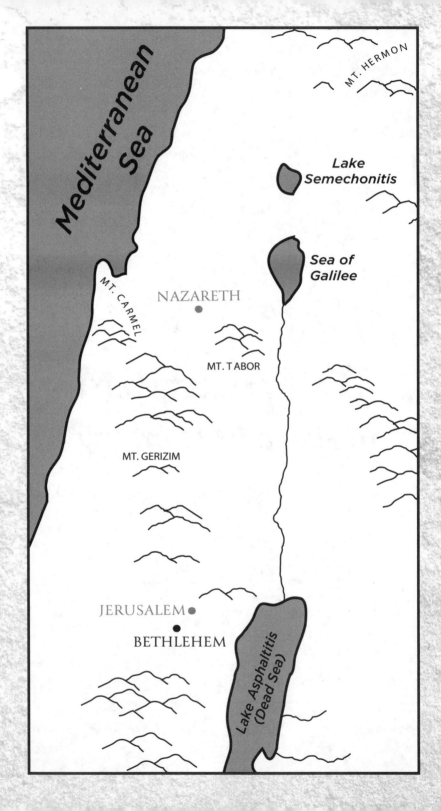

Introduction to Bethlehem

In Hebrew, the word Bethlehem means "house of bread." Perhaps this name derives from the agricultural character of the region. In the Book of Ruth, when Naomi returned to Bethlehem, we are told that it was during the barley harvest. Situated on a popular trade route between Egypt and northern provinces, Bethlehem was known for its bread.

More important is Bethlehem's spiritual meaning. This was the ancestral home of King David. David was promised by God that a future Messiah would come from his descendants. Isaiah 11:1 says, "A shoot shall come from the stump of Jesse." Jesse was David's father, and the shoot is a reference to the Anointed One. This is why Matthew and Luke, the only two Gospels to recount Jesus's birth, offer genealogies that trace his ancestry back to David. Therefore, Joseph had to travel with his betrothed wife to Bethlehem to register for the census that was ordered by Caesar Augustus because "he was descended from the house and family of David" (Luke 2:4).

Bethlehem today is a city of more than twenty-five thousand inhabitants, mostly Palestinian Muslims and Christians. The West Bank Wall, built by Israel in the early 2000s, separates Bethlehem from Jerusalem and other mostly Jewish areas. Tourism is the chief industry of Bethlehem, which receives over a million visitors each year. They come to see the place where Jesus was born and touch a rock believed to be part of the stable where Mary delivered Jesus that first Christmas. The grotto, where the access point to the stable is located, is beneath the beautiful Church of the Nativity and is believed to be the oldest site of continuous Christian worship. The first construction of a church on this site dates back to Constantine after his mother,

Helena, visited Bethlehem in the early fourth century. Since that time people have come to Bethlehem, just like the magi from the east, to pay homage to the Christ-child.

Just a few miles from the church is an eastern suburb of Bethlehem called Beit Sahur. This is the place where angels visited shepherds while watching over their flocks. A lookout over the hillsides helps visitors imagine shepherds grazing their sheep when they were interrupted by celestial guests. Close to this area is an Orthodox church, which commemorates the site referenced in Genesis 35:21 as "the tower of Edar," or the "tower of the flock." First posited by Eusebius, a church historian in the second century, this tower would have served as a logical place in which shepherds could have "watched over their flocks by night."

Not far from this point is a Catholic church that has a "chapel of angels" built beside it to mark the location of the shepherds' revelation. Steps from the chapel is a cave where, again, people have venerated a spot believed to have been a sheep stall.

Bethlehem has no shortage of places to worship or buy olive wood carvings. In spite of its popularity and tourism, Bethlehem still holds the mystique and awe of being the place where Jesus was born. Shepherds, angels, a young couple, a manger, and a baby are the participants in this incredible drama of divine love. This is why we came all this way.

CHAPTER 4
BETHLEHEM
A Place of Humility

In those days a decree went out from Caesar Augustus that all the world should be registered. This was the first registration and was taken while Quirinius was governor of Syria. All went to their own towns to be registered. Joseph also went from the town of Nazareth in Galilee to Judea, to the city of David called Bethlehem, because he was descended from the house and family of David. He went to be registered with Mary, to whom he was engaged and who was expecting a child. While they were there, the time came for her to deliver her child. And she gave birth to her firstborn son and wrapped him in bands of cloth and laid him in a manger, because there was no place in the guest room.

Now in that same region there were shepherds living in the fields, keeping watch over their flock by night. Then an angel of the Lord stood before them, and the glory of the Lord shone around them, and they were terrified. But the angel said to them, "Do not be afraid, for see, I am bringing you good news of great joy for all the people: to you is born this day in the city of David a Savior, who is the Messiah, the Lord. This will be a sign for you: you will find a child wrapped in bands of cloth and lying in a manger." And suddenly there was with the angel a multitude of the heavenly host, praising God and saying,

"Glory to God in the highest heaven,
and on earth peace among those whom he favors!"

When the angels had left them and gone into heaven, the shepherds said
to one another, "Let us go now to Bethlehem and see this thing that has
taken place, which the Lord has made known to us." So they went with
haste and found Mary and Joseph and the child lying in the manger.
When they saw this, they made known what had been told them about
this child, and all who heard it were amazed at what the shepherds told
them, and Mary treasured all these words and pondered them in her
heart. The shepherds returned, glorifying and praising God for all they
had heard and seen, just as it had been told them."

Luke 2:8-20

One Sunday morning in 1989, former president George H. W. Bush and his wife, Barbara, went to St. John's Episcopal Church just a few blocks from the White House. This is known as "the President's church" because of the many presidents who have worshipped there across the years. As the Bushes were about to enter, a homeless man named Wallace Brown said to the president, "Would you pray for me?" Mr. Bush stopped, looked at the man and replied, "No."

Now imagine if news crews had captured that moment. What might have become of such a story? Reporters may have left off the rest of what the president said to the man. He said, "No," but continued, "Why don't you come inside and pray for yourself?" And so the man walked in that morning. Mr. Brown would continue attending the church, eventually becoming a member.

He never missed a Sunday. A woman in the church who was a head usher said that everyone knew he was living on the streets. One Sunday she was going to politely skip Mr. Brown during the offering, but he stopped her and insisted on putting in the offering plate a wadded-up dollar bill. He did this every Sunday. She said, "Some of our wealthiest members only put in a dollar."

One Sunday a person refused to shake his hand during the passing of the peace. After the service, another member who observed this went to Brown and told him how upset it made him. But Brown said, "Don't worry, it's not an important thing." He wasn't angry about it.

Brown, though, could have spent his life being angry. He became homeless years before when he signed over his house to a lawyer who said he would help Brown get out of financial difficulty. It is believed that Brown was drunk at the time. He struggled with alcohol abuse. But instead of helping him, the lawyer sold the house and pocketed the money. Later a court found that Brown had been defrauded and ordered the lawyer to pay $50,000, but Brown refused it. All he wanted was his house back, but he never got it.

Through all his years of homelessness, he never took another drink. His involvement in the church brought him happiness and peace. He endeared himself to the congregation. When he died his unclaimed body would have been buried in what is known as "the potter's field" in Washington. But the members of the church petitioned and were granted to have legal claim to his remains as his spiritual next of kin. They interred him in a sacred columbarium next to the church where fewer than one hundred people have been so honored since the church was built in 1816.[1]

The story of how Mr. Brown came to be buried at St. John's Episcopal Church in Washington, DC, all started when a person of high authority invited someone of low estate to have his own connection to God. How much more significant is the news that the one who is in highest authority, the Maker of heaven and earth, should meet us as a baby born in a cattle stall? What meaning can we take from this fact and the events surrounding the birth of Jesus? The answers to these questions are what bring us at last to the final stop on our journey to Christmas: Bethlehem.

Why Bethlehem?

Before answering those questions and discussing the conditions surrounding Jesus's birth, let's first consider a more fundamental question, why Bethlehem? Why is this village the place where Jesus was born? The political answer, of course, is Rome. Caesar Augustus issued a decree for a census to be taken throughout the Roman world. As mentioned in the first chapter, this decree was probably given before Mary was visited by the angel Gabriel, when she came to be with child. Without speedy communication systems like today, it may have taken more than a year before people were going to a village like Bethlehem to register for a census. Why Mary and Joseph had a baby in Bethlehem is because of events in Rome that may have taken place before Mary was even expecting.

The political answer to the question, though, doesn't give the full answer. There is a religious explanation as well. Joseph had to go back to the place of his ancestral heritage. Joseph was a descendant of David from whom the future Messiah would come. The prophet Jeremiah foretold, "I will raise up for David a righteous Branch, and he shall reign as king and deal wisely and shall execute justice and righteousness in the land" (23:5). Both Matthew and Luke include genealogies that clearly trace the heritage of Jesus's earthly father, Joseph, back to David. Because Bethlehem was Joseph's ancestral home as a descendant of David, Joseph and Mary were required to travel there from Nazareth to enroll for the census.

But, still, how did Bethlehem get established as the ancestral home of David? To find out, we have to go all the way back in the Old Testament to the Book of Ruth. This is where we learn the secret behind Bethlehem as the place where Jesus was born. Ruth is the beautiful story of a Moabite girl who married a Jewish man whose family lived in her country. Her mother-in-law was a devout Jewish woman named Naomi. Shortly after Naomi's husband died, so did her son, Ruth's husband, as well as her other son, whose wife was named Orpah.

Naomi told her bereaved daughters-in-law that she was going to return to her home country, and they should return to their families of origin. After all, they were still young enough to remarry and have families of their own. After putting up initial resistance to leaving Naomi, Orpah relented and returned to her home. But Ruth refused Naomi's request. She vowed to stay by Naomi's side, speaking words that may sound familiar: "Where you go, I will go; where you lodge, I will lodge; your people shall be my people and your God my God" (Ruth 1:16). We sometimes hear this scripture read at weddings, but the words weren't spoken by two people about to be married. They were spoken urgently by a young woman to her mother-in-law, both of whom were united in grief.

Together Naomi and Ruth returned to Naomi's hometown of Bethlehem. They were without resources, so to help make ends meet Ruth found a field where hired pickers were gleaning the produce. The workers allowed her to go behind them and gather from what was left. In Leviticus it says, "When you reap the harvest of your land, you shall not reap to the very edges of your field or gather the gleanings of your harvest; you shall leave them for the poor and for the alien (23:22). The Torah commands people to provide for the poor and the stranger. Ruth fit the description of a resident foreigner, so the fact that she was allowed to glean in this field meant its owner was obedient to the commands of Torah Law.

The owner, as it turns out, was a relative of Naomi. His name was Boaz. He learned Ruth's story and how she refused to leave Naomi. He showed compassion for Ruth, telling his workers to protect her, allowing her to glean even from the main harvest, and offering her plenty to eat at mealtime. That evening when Naomi asked Ruth where she had gleaned that day, she told her the whole story. When Ruth mentioned the name of the man who owned the field and showed her kindness, Naomi responded, "Blessed be he by the Lord, whose kindness has not forsaken the living or the dead!" (Ruth 2:20) Naomi praised God and her response is worth a brief consideration.

The last time Naomi referenced God in regard to her plight following the deaths of her husband and two sons, she said, "The hand of the Lord has turned against me" (Ruth 1:13). Her faith was filtered through her circumstances. This is not a judgment on Naomi. How many of us wouldn't feel God was against us if we faced the same losses? Pain and adversity can cloud our ability to experience the presence of God.

Now, however, the circumstances have changed. When Naomi learns that the man who took compassion on Ruth was named Boaz, she not only celebrates his kindness, but she also celebrates the kindness of God. Just as painful realities can block our ability to see God's hand at work, the opposite can be true as well. Simple acts of mercy or unexpected blessings can be claimed as evidence of God's love in action.

Have you been through a season of pain in your life? Have circumstances weathered your faith? At the same time, have there been acts of mercy or blessings to celebrate? Those blessings might not equal the loss you've suffered, but they could signal a shift, a movement that points toward the fact that God has not forgotten you and is at work to give you a future and a hope (Jeremiah 29:11).

Little Hope

Author Joyce Hollyday tells about a teacher who had a very specialized assignment, teaching students who had prolonged hospital stays. She would receive lessons from the students' teachers and then go to the hospital rooms to tutor the students. One assignment was to work with a student on his nouns and adverbs. She knew nothing about his condition until arriving at his room in the burn center. She discovered he had been badly burned and was in intense pain. She composed herself and announced to the student that her teacher wanted him to work on nouns and adverbs. The boy could barely speak, and it was all the tutor could do to stay focused. She felt terrible for making the boy endure such a senseless exercise.

The next morning a nurse asked the tutor, "What did you do to that boy?" Before she could begin her litany of apologies, the nurse explained, "We've been very worried about him. But ever since you were here yesterday, his whole attitude has changed. He's fighting back; he's responding to treatment. It's as if he has decided to live."

The boy later admitted that he had indeed given up hope until he met the teacher. He said, "They wouldn't send a teacher to help me work on nouns and adverbs if I was going to die!"[2]

Sometimes great hope comes in little signs.

I don't know anyone who would turn down an answer to prayer, but what if that answer didn't come in one lump serving? What if it came in bite-sized portions, that could, if accepted, lead to bigger

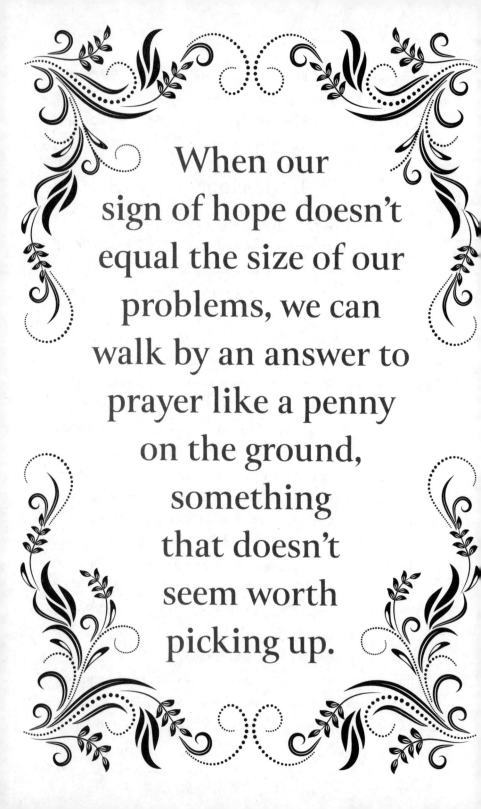

When our
sign of hope doesn't
equal the size of our
problems, we can
walk by an answer to
prayer like a penny
on the ground,
something
that doesn't
seem worth
picking up.

ones? When our sign of hope doesn't equal the size of our problems, we can walk by an answer to prayer like a penny on the ground, something that doesn't seem worth picking up.

Jesus's Family History

Naomi was finding new joy and hope in her return to Bethlehem, but not just for the kindness of a stranger. Naomi told Ruth, "The man is a relative of ours, one of our nearest kin" (Ruth 2:20). That is a most important statement, but before delving into the "nearest kin" reference, notice how Naomi no longer talks to Ruth as someone who should go back to "her people." She speaks to Ruth as someone who shares her family history. Bethlehem, it turns out, is not only a place where faith is restored, but also a place where everyone is included in God's provision and hope.

Now back to the nearest-kin comment. Boaz was not just a relative, he was known as a "kinsman-redeemer." This was another provision in the Torah for Israelites, especially women, who fell on hard times and lost their property. In such an instance the nearest male relative served as a redeemer. As it says in Leviticus 25:25: "If anyone of your kin falls into difficulty and sells a piece of property, then the next of kin shall come and redeem what the relative has sold."

Naomi gave Ruth some crafty advice on how to win over Boaz's affection, which Ruth did. As a kinsman-redeemer, Boaz would be able to take Ruth as his wife. This is where the story involves some added drama. Boaz was a redeemer-relative, but not the nearest one. Another man was closer in line, so Boaz met the man in the village square and informed him that he is the nearest redeemer-relative to buy back property originally owned by Naomi. At first the man was interested, then Boaz informed him that claiming his right as redeemer also included Ruth. The man would have to make Ruth his wife. Being a redeemer was not just a material matter, it was relational as well. The man said this would complicate matters of inheritance in his own family, so he forfeited his right of redemption and passed it onto Boaz.

Boaz and Ruth marry and have a son. The women of the village say to Naomi, "May the Lord be blessed, who today hasn't left you without a redeemer" (Ruth 4:14 CEB). The story says the women of Bethlehem named the child. There was obviously a sense in which this child belonged to everyone in Bethlehem. They gave him the name Obed. Obed became the father of Jesse who became the father of David, the king who was promised by God to have an heir one day who would be the Messiah. The story ends with Naomi holding her grandson. Bethlehem was a place of new life and redemption.

This is how Bethlehem came to be associated with David as his ancestral home. Given that the promise of a future Messiah came from the line of David, it is interesting to note that David's own grandmother, Ruth, was not Jewish. She was a Moabite widow who depended on provisions in the Torah for the welfare of the poor and foreigners.

Bethlehem represents Jesus's family history, a history that came about because a foreigner received compassion. Jesus's DNA contains racial ethnicity, immigrant assistance, religious faithfulness, and loving mercy. No wonder he said and did the things he did. Jesus showed compassion for Samaritans, people who were racial outcasts at the time. Jesus even suggested in the parable of the Good Samaritan that they are to be considered as neighbors. Most Jewish people would have considered only fellow Israelites as neighbors, people to whom they were responsible to show compassion. Jesus also showed mercy on a widow in the village of Nain by bringing her dead son back to life. In the parable of the Sheep and Goats, Jesus said, "I was hungry and you gave me food; I was thirsty and you gave me drink; I was a stranger and you welcomed me" (Matthew 25:35). Bethlehem, it turns out, provides some clues as to the character and values Jesus would display as a Messiah.

Among the Little

With that historical background on Bethlehem, let's look at one other Old Testament reference that helps us answer the question, why Bethlehem? The prophet Micah, in predicting the future hope of Israel, declared:

> But you, O Bethlehem of Ephrathah,
>   who are one of the little clans of Judah,
> from you shall come forth for me
>   one who is to rule in Israel,
> whose origin is from of old,
>   from ancient days.
>
> Micah 5:2

Bethlehem was considered "one of the little clans of Judah." This description is reminiscent of the words of Gideon. When an angel appeared to him one day with the command to lead Israel in fighting the Midianites, Gideon responded, "My clan is the weakest...and I am the least in my family" (Judges 6:15). The way we see ourselves is often revealed by the challenges we face. Greatness is not something we give ourselves. It is something we have to receive.

In spite of Bethlehem's ancestral connection to King David, it was still viewed as a little place, which may be an added reason God chose Bethlehem as the place for Jesus to be born. Jesus came to identify with the least of society. In his first sermon in the Gospel of Matthew, Jesus's opening words were, "Blessed are the poor in spirit, for theirs is the kingdom of heaven" (Matthew 5:3). In Luke's Gospel Jesus just said, "Blessed are you who are poor" (Luke 6:20). Jesus healed lepers whose condition excluded them from participation in the life of the community. He protected a woman whom the religious leaders were ready to execute because of adultery. His parables like the prodigal son and his brother, the good Samaritan, and the widow and the unjust judge all show compassion for people many would have deemed unworthy or unimportant. He extended grace to a notorious tax collector, Zacchaeus, as well as the thief on the cross. Bethlehem foreshadowed the many ways Jesus would give attention to those who were among the little in society.

Welcoming the Least

With that bit of Old Testament background establishing the significance of Bethlehem, we are ready for a stop just outside the village, the Shepherds' Fields. This region marks the place where the angel visited shepherds as they watched over their flocks that first Christmas night. The angel declared,

> *I am bringing you good news of great joy for all the people: to you is born this day in the city of David a Savior, who is the Messiah, the Lord. This will be a sign for you: you will find a child wrapped in bands of cloth and lying in a manger."*
>
> *Luke 2:10-12*

These shepherds were the first ones invited to greet Jesus after he was born. Shepherds would have been a common sight in and around Bethlehem. Many of the lambs raised for sacrifice at the Temple likely came from surrounding regions such as Bethlehem. The nearest entrance through the city wall to the Temple was known as the Sheep's Gate, which today is the Lion's Gate. This is where the sheep used for sacrificial worship were brought to the Temple. To the right of this gate, once you entered, was a pool where the sheep were washed and prepared. This became known as the Sheep's Pool, the place where Jesus healed a man who had been lame for thirty-eight years (John 5).

But just what role do shepherds play in the birth story? Opinions are divided. Some point out the many noble references to shepherding in the Old Testament. God was often described as a shepherd. David said, "The Lord is my shepherd" (Psalm 23:1). Isaiah said that God's relationship to his people is like that of a shepherd to his sheep:

He will feed his flock like a shepherd;
    he will gather the lambs in his arms
and carry them in his bosom
    and gently lead the mother sheep.
                    Isaiah 40:11

Jeremiah said much the same:

Then I myself will gather the remnant of my flock out of all the lands where I have driven them, and I will bring them back to their fold, and they shall be fruitful and multiply. I will raise up shepherds over them who will shepherd them, and they shall no longer fear or be dismayed, nor shall any be missing, says the LORD.
                    Jeremiah 23:3-4

And God said through the prophet Ezekiel:

As shepherds sort out their flocks when they are among scattered sheep, so
I will sort out my sheep. I will rescue them from all the places to which
they have been scattered on a day of clouds and thick darkness.

Ezekiel 34:12

Even Jesus called himself the "good shepherd" (John 10:11). Shepherding language found its way into modern church vocabulary. The word "pastor" comes from the Latin word for shepherd. Scholar Amy-Jill Levine writes, "Contrary to some Christian teaching, Jews of the time did not view shepherds as outcasts or unclean."[3]

The Bible, however, also shows less admirable attitudes toward shepherding. In the Book of Genesis, when Joseph's family moved to Egypt to escape famine, they lived in the land of Goshen, apart from other Egyptians, because "all shepherds are abhorrent to the Egyptians" (46:34). Not everyone treated shepherds nobly. Even Jesus contrasted his being a "good shepherd" with "hirelings," shepherds who didn't own their flocks but were hired to care for them. When threats like wild animals or bandits came along, hirelings were quick to abandon their flocks. Not all shepherds were good.

New Testament professor Alan Culpepper says that shepherding was a despised occupation at the time and "shepherds were scorned as shiftless, dishonest people who grazed their flocks on others' lands."[4] In Adam Hamilton's book on Luke's Gospel, he recognizes a derogatory term used in the first century, "Am ha-Arez," which meant "people of the land."[5] It was a label meant to mock those who were not among the educated or religious elite of the day. Certainly, shepherds were considered among the people of the land.

Why the difference of opinion? How could the same people be so respected on the one hand and be viewed with contempt on the other? An experience I had in college might make some sense of this contradiction.

To earn spending money while at school I had a job working in the cafeteria. Most of the time I washed dishes, which was inglorious work. Fortunately, the counter where students brought their trays after a meal had a low opening so people couldn't see your face, just your hands reaching out to take their dirty plates and utensils. It was one of those jobs where you were glad for people not to know who you were. But every now and then, I got to do other kinds of work, like catering food service events on the campus. Often these events were at the president's house where he and his wife hosted special functions.

One night I got to be a guest at the president's house. They hosted a catered reception for students with special academic achievement that semester. I put on a tie and wore the only dress coat I had. The president's wife was at the door greeting each student as we arrived. She read my name tag and later in the evening called me by name without having to look down at my tag. She asked what I was studying, where I was from, and inquired about my family.

The very next night I was back at the president's house but this time in a food service capacity. I wore the same tie, only now it was mostly covered by an apron. I came in through the back door carrying several trays into the kitchen. The president's wife was standing there. I said to her, "Good evening Mrs. So-and-So." She looked at me with no glint of recognition and said, "Just put those over there and then come this way. I need your help." I honestly believe she had no idea that I was the same young man she took such an interest in the night before. Now she gave orders in a very testy manner, looking displeased that I didn't know exactly where to find things in the kitchen.

I went back to my dorm room feeling embarrassed and even mad. Then I thought, "Wait a minute. I didn't change. I am the same person as I was the night before." Then I felt as if God said to me in that moment, "You are right, Rob. You are the same person. Remember this, because people will look at others by what they see on the outside, but everyone is a child of mine worthy of treating with respect." Once I got beyond my personal feelings, I was grateful for what became an important teaching moment.

I believe that is why God invited the shepherds to be the first to adore the Christ child, to restore to them the honor and dignity that was their heritage. Think for a moment about a few of the people who weren't at the stable. The High Priest, who represented the entire faith system that prophesied this Messiah's coming, wasn't there. Neither were the government officials like Herod, Quirinius, or Caesar Augustus who represented worldly power. None of them were there. Certainly, their presence would have given credibility to the significance of Jesus's birth, except people don't make the birth of Jesus credible. It's the other way around!

Shepherds are in the story of Christmas because even though they possessed a proud identity and noble heritage, they lived in a world in which others could erode that pride and nobility. They were the first congregation to praise God for the Christ-child because they represented God's desire to come and restore people. Restore them to their true selves. Restore them from the prejudiced attitudes and treatment of others. Restore the very character of God in them.

We live in a world in which people value others for what others can do for them. Just look at the adoring crowds gathered around people of fame and fortune. Association with important people makes us feel important. Yet when celebrities fall from grace or cease producing hit songs, new blockbusters, or more championships, the adoring crowds diminish. Such adoration reveals how we never sought the person, just the perception of that person.

The Christmas story reminds us that we're all shepherds at heart. Our adoration is meant to be reserved for the only One who can restore in us the value we desperately desire. God's blessing is reserved for the lowly. That is not a statement of class distinction as if God blesses only the poor or marginalized. It is a statement of spiritual distinction. God blesses those who recognize their need to be blessed. God blesses those who understand their need for God is more important than wealth, success, or recognition. The shepherds serve as a testimony to Mary's Magnificat, "He has brought down the powerful from their thrones and lifted up the lowly; he has filled the hungry with good things and sent the rich away empty" (Luke 1:52-53). This prophecy would be realized in Jesus's life. Those most blessed by Jesus are those most willing to depend on him.

The Church of the Nativity in Bethlehem has a giant door at the main entrance, but within it is another door just four feet high. It is called the "Door of Humility." There are several stories associated with how this door came to be. One goes back to the days of the crusades. Knights would come to receive a blessing from the priest before going to battle. The ritual became so routine the knights stopped bothering to dismount from their horses. In fact, they eventually just rode their horses through the large entrance into the sanctuary so they could be blessed and get on their way. Their behavior outraged the priest. He boarded up the entrance and cut a small door that would require the knights to get off their horses and crawl into the church. The message was clear, if you want a blessing, you have to get on your knees.

God blesses those
who recognize their
need to be blessed.
God blesses those
who understand their
need for God
is more important
than wealth, success,
or recognition.

One Last Thought on Shepherds

Before we leave the shepherds' fields and head into the village of Bethlehem, let's consider one last thought. The shepherds didn't just receive a blessing, they gave one. They had an experience of glory to share.

The only glory Mary received on Christmas night was surviving the delivery. She nor Joseph received an ecstatic vision or heavenly display. For them, the first Christmas up to that point probably involved more questions and uncertainty than it did faith. I can imagine Mary, after giving birth, being physically and emotionally exhausted. Seeing her son lying on a bed of straw, not in a home, not on a bed, not aided by loved ones or a midwife, I can picture her breaking into tears. She and Joseph both could have wondered, "Did we get something wrong? We both heard from angels. We have been obedient. So, what are we doing here? If this is God's Son, why wouldn't God have looked after us better? Have we been abandoned?"

The Bible, of course, gives no indication of this, but the thoughts and feelings seem reasonable, which means the arrival of the shepherds would not have been just for their own benefit. Their testimony of what the angel said, and the experience of a heavenly choir singing, "Glory to God in the highest heaven, and on earth peace among those whom [God] favors" (Luke 2:14), no doubt gave assurance to Mary and Joseph. No wonder Luke reports that after hearing the shepherds' story, "Mary treasured all these words and pondered them in her heart." (Luke 2:19) Because the shepherds were obedient to their vision from God, they were able to provide comfort and confidence to Mary and Joseph.

Has God given you any promptings to go to others and witness to the godliness you see in them? You never know how you might be an echo of God's voice in their lives. Also, what does it mean to be a blessing to fellow shepherds—people whose true identity can get eroded by the world? What does it mean to treat others based solely on the blessing you want to give them and not the blessing you want from them?

A Stable Place

At last, we arrive at our final destination on this journey to Christmas: the stable. Even though Bethlehem was a small place, our destination is more specific than the town itself. We must find our way to the stable. This is much harder than it sounds. Most stables were out of sight. Some were attached to the rear of homes, a pen bordered by a rock wall or wooden fence. Other stables were actually inside the homes. Finding the stable requires active seeking.

There are only two facts given about the location of Jesus's birth. First, he was laid in a manger, a feeding trough for animals. This is why we associate his birth as happening in a stable where animals were kept. Second, there was no room in the inn.

This second fact has led to all kinds of speculation. Tradition assumes that the inn was a lodging place like a Motel 6, just without the light left on. However, no such inns existed in the ancient world, especially in small villages like Bethlehem. Picture something more like a small Bed and Breakfast, a private home in which guest rooms were rented. In fact, "guest room" is the actual translation of the word commonly given as "inn."

If the events of Christmas started in Rome, that could mean God orchestrated all along for Jesus to be born in a stable. Think about it. If God intended for Jesus to born in Bethlehem at a time when the village would be crowded, God must have meant for Mary and Joseph to end up in a stable. Now, I'll confess this doesn't fit my theology so well. I don't believe God scripts every event in life just the way it happens. Yet, for the sake of imagination and argument, let's suppose the exact location of Jesus's birth was all according to God's plan.

Even if you can't quite go there, just ask yourself why the stable and inn are even mentioned. The story could fittingly be told, "And (Mary) gave birth to her firstborn son and wrapped him in bands of cloth." Period! Why mention anything about laying him in a manger because there was no room in the inn. At least for the Gospel writer Luke, there seems to be an important reason for adding this detail.

So, what's the purpose of the stable?

My father-in-law is Bishop Richard Wilke, author of *Disciple Bible Study*. He is an amazing preacher and passionate church leader to whom I am honored to be a son-in-law. Before Susan and I were married, we spent our first Christmas together visiting her parents in Little Rock where her dad was the United Methodist Bishop of Arkansas. I saw a copy of their conference newsletter which had a bishop's column. I kept it and have saved it all these years. My father-in-law shared the words written by a friend of his, an Episcopal priest named Morton Kelsey:

> Where was the Christ-child born? Where I ask you? In a palace amid the splendors of servants and the comforts of ease? Was he received on a silken pillow and adored by all the glittering household? No, he wasn't born in a palace and I am glad for it; for had he been born there I could not hope that he could be born in my life; in my soul, because my soul is no palace.

> Was Jesus born in the inn, in a swept and garnished room with an attendant to help the mother in labor? No! All the world knows there was no room in the inn, and I am thankful...because my

soul, my heart, is not swept, comfortable and orderly. If the Christ-child needs a well-kept hotel in which to be born, then he couldn't be born in me.[6]

Kelsey goes on to talk about a legend regarding the stable and how strangers would come to find shelter there, how a runaway shepherd who killed his master came there to hide, how on another night a drunken soldier staggered there and fell asleep, and how on yet another night a prostitute weary of her life went there to find escape and solitude. Kelsey concludes: "Such was the place where Christ was born, and it is great consolation to me and to every honest person, for my soul is more like the stable—with animal instincts and strange inhabitants—than it is a palace or an inn."[7]

Carl Sandburg said, "A baby is God's opinion that the world should go on."[8] In the case of Jesus, God's opinion is more than just the world going on as it is. This baby was born to make the world a better place. Jesus's first cradle was a symbol that the world needed improvement. The manger was a messy place. This was an unsuitable place for a baby. Much of our world is not suited for godly habitation. Our world is messy. There is child abuse, spousal abuse, racism, sex exploitation, human trafficking, drugs, gun violence, corrupt governments, intolerance of those with different opinions or appearance. You name it.

Yet God chose to be born in a manger. God comes to the places where we need God, not where we are doing a pretty good job ourselves keeping life tidied up so things look presentable. No, God meets us in our sin. Sin is what damages the soul, and what damages the soul impairs the world. Sin goes beyond bad choices. Sin becomes crippling behavior. It spills over into our relationships. Sin becomes greed, racism, sexism, slavery, hatred, violence, and so on.

We picture the manger as a tender place, but make no mistake, it is a volatile invasion. The kingdom of God comes near in this manger. God is still in charge and will not quit. God does not give up. What happened in this tiny, dirty, remote location is the beginning of a rightsizing of the world. The Maker of heaven and earth has stepped into history, but God comes not with sword drawn or armies charging. God doesn't come first to the halls of congress or parliaments. God comes as a frail baby needing care and love. God comes to every person who would open their arms to embrace him, not just because this baby needs our care, but because we need God's.

Is it time to dismount from some high horse and get on your knees? The power of the Christmas story comes down to each person admitting their need for God's grace and help. God's mother and father stand outside our door needing a place for their child to be born. We are the innkeepers of our souls, which means we all have mangers. We don't need to pretend we don't. That's where God seeks to come. Will you open your arms to God?

"Will you pray for me?" said Mr. Brown to the president of the United States. "No," responded the president. "Why don't you come inside and pray for yourself." And the two men worshipped together. Someone in highest authority met someone at his lowest, and a future was altered.

"The shepherds returned, glorifying and praising God for all they had heard and seen, just as it had been told them" (Luke 2:20).

Amen.

EPILOGUE

PERSIA

Place of Return

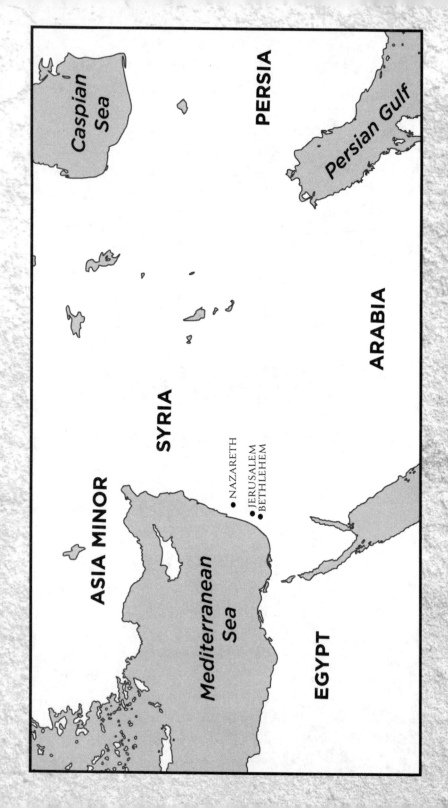

EPILOGUE
PERSIA
Place of Return

In the time of King Herod, after Jesus was born in Bethlehem of Judea, magi from the east came to Jerusalem asking, "Where is the child who has been born king of the Jews? For we observed his star in the east and have come to pay him homage." When King Herod heard this, he was frightened, and all Jerusalem with him, and calling together all the chief priests and scribes of the people, he inquired of them where the Messiah was to be born. They told him, "In Bethlehem of Judea, for so it has been written by the prophet:

> *'And you, Bethlehem, in the land of Judah,*
> > *are by no means least among the rulers of Judah,*
> *for from you shall come a ruler*
> > *who is to shepherd my people Israel.'"*

Then Herod secretly called for the magi and learned from them the exact time when the star had appeared. Then he sent them to Bethlehem, saying, "Go and search diligently for the child, and when you have found him, bring me word so that I may also go and pay him homage." When they had heard the king, they set out, and there, ahead of them, went the star that they had seen in the east, until it stopped over the place where the child was. When they saw that the star had stopped, they were overwhelmed with joy. On entering the house, they saw the child with Mary his mother, and they knelt down and paid him homage. Then, opening their treasure chests, they offered him gifts of gold, frankincense, and myrrh. And having been warned in a dream not to return to Herod, they left for their own country by another road.

Matthew 2:1-12

There are many ways to take a journey. You can pack a bag and get on a plane. You can get in the car and drive somewhere. You can walk around your neighborhood. Sometimes reading a good book is like taking a journey. We speak of walking with loved ones through journeys of grief or illness. Each day itself is like a journey, offering conversations, encounters, and opportunities to learn or grow.

Journeys can be broad and varied, but all journeys usually involve a starting place, various experiences along the way, and usually a return. Perhaps there are some journeys that don't bring us back to where we started. They permanently take us to new locations, whether that be physical places or emotional ones. But most of the time our journeys return to where we started, but this doesn't mean they return us the same as we started. Journeys always change us. Often we are not even conscious of the changes. We meet people who become a lasting part of our lives. We have experiences that expand us and perhaps affect our understanding of cultures and places. Perhaps we bring back new discoveries we want to make a permanent part of who we are. Whether we are aware of them or not our journeys shape us.

As I mentioned earlier in this book, I am just weeks away from taking a three-month sabbatical, the longest in my thirty-five-plus years of ministry. A few months back I spoke with a colleague who took a sabbatical several years ago. I asked what advice he could give me as I prepare for this adventure. He said, "People will tell you to plan your sabbatical well, plan how to manage your time and things like email so you don't get dragged into work-mode. Plan activities that will maximize your sense of escape, and so on. But," he continued, "I would say the most important thing you can do is plan your return carefully."

I asked him to say more.

He explained, "When my sabbatical ended, I just jumped back into work like I was the same person without thinking what was different about me. Who was the different *me* I was bringing home and back to the church? It was like I was force fitting a changed personality into an old pattern."

I made a note to self: a good return will be an important key to a good journey. As we close our Advent journey, let's consider the last visitors to arrive in Bethlehem to worship the Christ-child and what they have to teach us about returning from a spiritual journey.

The Journey of the Magi

The magi are the last characters in the Christmas story to make their way to Bethlehem. Some scholars estimate that the magi arrived as much as one to two years after Jesus's birth. Notice one detail in Matthew's account: "On entering the *house* they saw the child with Mary his mother" (2:11). At some point after Jesus was born, Mary and Joseph found a home in which to stay in Bethlehem. They may have even been at this home when Jesus was born, but because the guest room (the same word that is translated "inn") was taken, they stayed in the stable. This could have been the home of Joseph's relatives. Once their guests vacated the guest room, Mary and Joseph (and Jesus) moved in. One thing for certain, though, is that the wise men were not at the stable.

Also, the Bible doesn't mention how many magi there were or that they were kings. So now that I've ruined the idea of wise men being in Nativity scenes, as well as our hymn "We Three Kings," let's consider what we actually know. Matthew tells us that these magi traveled some distance "from the east" to pay homage to a king of the Jews whose birth they saw in a natal star. This gives us some insight as to who these strange figures were. They were people who studied the stars, like ancient astronomers, but their reading signs of human events in the stars is what leads many historians to call them astrologers. Scholars differ on where the magi were from. Some say they were magicians from the empire of the Medes, central Asia. Others say they came from a country closer to the Mediterranean region. Most agree they came from Persia, modern-day Iran, and were likely priests of the Zoroastrian religion.

Zoroastrianism is the oldest monotheistic faith still in practice in the world. It was started three thousand years ago by Zoroaster, also known as Zarathustra, in Persia before the rise of Islam. Zoroastrians believe in a never-ending battle between good and evil and that believers are free to make good and bad choices. Perhaps the magi were devoted seekers after good and looked to the stars for divine guidance.

The Original Seekers

The expression "seekers" has faded out of popular use among evangelical Christians today. The label refers to people who identify themselves as spiritual but not religious. This was a way of recognizing people who were looking for something but not sure what. I suppose you could call the magi the original seekers, only they knew what they were looking for. Whatever they saw in the star of Bethlehem, they took it as a sign that a king of the Jews had been born.

In this sense the star of Bethlehem doesn't so much represent the magi's seeking as it does their finding. They must have already been seeking in order to have noticed the star in the first place. You have to wonder just how obvious and noticeable the star of Bethlehem was. When the magi arrived in Jerusalem to inquire from the local ruler, King Herod, if he knew anything about the birth of a new king, he and his whole court seemed completely unaware. We picture the star in many of our manger scenes as being an unmistakable sign. Scholarly attempts have been made to identify an astronomical event of the time period that may explain what the magi saw.

William Barclay recognizes a number of these, including a rare alignment of the planets Saturn and Jupiter around 7 BC, as well as an unknown extraordinary stellar event between 5 BC and 2 BC.[1] But if the star of Bethlehem was some brilliantly visible sign, why were there no other people in the story who saw it? Could it be that the star was fainter than we imagine? Rather than being an irrefutable sign pointing the way to Bethlehem, what if it was visible just to those who were seeking?

This raises a good question for consideration when it comes to planning a good return. What are you seeking? Notice the question is not, what should you be seeking? Keep the answer practical, real, and honest. What are you really seeking in your life right now? If you're not sure, then consider where you put most of your time and energy. Is it work? Are your thoughts typically consumed with opportunities and problems in your work life? If an honest answer is maybe, then what does that mean? Could the drive, or overdrive, for work reveal something you are inwardly seeking like reward, success, recognition, fulfillment, or something else?

Are you seeking approval? Do you find yourself seeking acceptance among friends and peers? Do you long for a sense of value from certain people?

Do you seek escape? Do you find yourself frequently daydreaming about the next vacation or getaway. When you go on vacation do you spend time planning the next vacation? What does that seeking reveal?

Do you seek tranquility in relationships? Do you find yourself having a hard time sleeping at night worrying about a family flare-up or a squabble with a neighbor? Is the political division among friends, colleagues, or fellow church members taking a toll on you?

Mind you, all of us are usually seeking something, if not many things, at any given time. You could say we are born seekers. The Bible says God "has planted eternity in the human heart" (Ecclesiastes 3:11 NLT). We are made to search for more in life, and it is part of our human condition to have a longing for satisfaction and yet have trouble being fully satisfied at the same time. This side of heaven, though, we will always long for more because the perfect has not yet come.

Seeking isn't bad, it's where our seeking can take us that becomes problematic. Sometimes our seeking can lead to unsatisfying solutions. Sometimes our drive for satisfaction just makes us selfish, always pursuing our own happiness. Seeking and wanting more in life isn't bad as long as we take our yearnings to God.

If the star of Bethlehem may not have been noticeable to most people, then that means we have to carefully and earnestly seek God's direction. Such seeking requires effort and willingness. After all, the magi had to look up to see the star. Think of looking up in a metaphorical way. How might you practice a looking-up pattern of living? If you believe that God is real, and that God is active and at work, then how can you practice a routine of looking for God's signs?

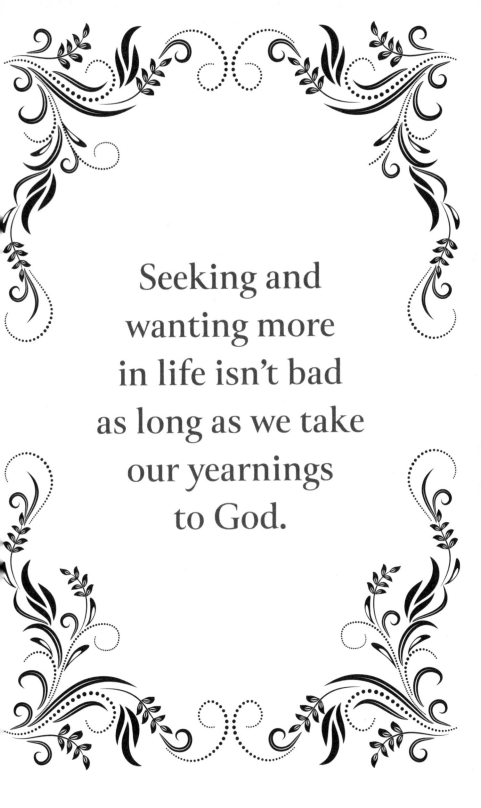

Seeking and
wanting more
in life isn't bad
as long as we take
our yearnings
to God.

My former bishop, the late Mike Coyner, used to have his cabinet take time in their meetings to acknowledge "Glory-Sightings," stories of how they have witnessed God at work. He said too much of the time we can lapse into "Gory-sightings," naming all the problems and obstacles to the work of God. In positions like a bishop and district superintendents have, this is something they see a lot. Therefore, as Coyner implored them and all clergy, we have to be intentional about seeking Glory.

I wonder if the magi saw something in the sky no one else did, because they were looking for divine activity. How might you practice a looking-up style of faith?

Earlier we were invited to reflect on where we are this Advent. What have we brought into this season? Identifying our longings, how we are waiting on God, where our lives need to simplify, and what humility could yield for us are all important questions that help us define our place in life. This journey to Bethlehem, however, doesn't just involve *our* place. We have been on a journey to meet God. God is in this place with us. That's the point of going to Bethlehem, to understand and better recognize God's place among us. Experiencing God's presence, or just being open to the idea that God is present with us, begins to change how we see ourselves and where we are. If our journey includes God, then we must take God's needs, wants, and preferences into account. God is a lot more than a chauffeur waiting for us to answer the question of "Where would you like to go?" God is the conductor saying, "Welcome aboard, our next stop will be..." So, as you return from this journey, how is your faith different?

Re-Turning versus Returning

A good return is an important key to a good journey. That is true, but something else is true as well. If all we did was return without re-turning, then all we've done is start over instead of start new. This is what change management expert, William Bridges, identifies as the difference between change and transition. Change is situational, the shifts of people and structures around us—a new boss, a staff restructuring, a closed office. Transition, on the other hand, is psychological, how we choose to face and move through change.[2]

A theological word that signifies transition is repentance. Some Christians weigh down the understanding of repentance with notions of guilt, shame, and feeling remorseful about one's failures. Repentance, however, comes from the Greek word *metanoia*, which means to change one's mind or direction—or both. Repentance is about choosing, by God's help, to turn and go in a new or different direction.

Repentance is the mark of a significant spiritual experience. Because we have been encountered by the God who is always doing a new thing, we are invited to do the same. This means repentance is not a one-time event, as if our coming to faith was the only time God invites us to change course. God is always on the move. God routinely leads us to new places, places in our beliefs, attitudes, and actions. Thus, the spiritual life is a series of re-turning, turning in new directions over and over again.

The Magi's Re-turn Home

King Herod was an insecure king who would not tolerate the idea of a future threat to his throne. His own track record was evidence. He murdered one of his wives along with her mother and grandfather as well as three of his sons. When Herod first learned from the magi about the birth of a King of the Jews, he was frightened, "and all Jerusalem with him" (Matthew 2:3). When a troubled king becomes afraid, so is everyone else. So, Herod discerns from his advisors that the future Messiah will come from Bethlehem and sends the magi on their way, asking that when they find the child, they *return* so that he too can worship the Christ-child.

After the magi left Herod, the star reappeared directing them to the home where Jesus was. Upon seeing him, they bowed in worship, then presented their gifts of gold, frankincense, and myrrh, all very costly, valuable items. With their mission accomplished, the magi were ready to begin their long journey home but being warned in a dream not to *return* to Herod, "they left for their own country by another road" (Matthew 2:12).

Notice the way the word "return" appears in this story. First, Herod told the magi to *return* to him, pretending he wanted to worship Jesus as well, but inwardly his heart was intent on harm. Herod's problem was that nothing had changed in his heart. He was still insecure, fearful, and willing to kill to protect his own position. All Herod did through his whole life was keep returning to the same person he had always been. Never did he re-turn and go a different way.

Second, the magi are warned not to *return* to Herod, and they heeded the angel's direction. Had they not gone home a different way, Jesus's life would have been endangered and they would have unwittingly been accomplices to his murder by Herod. But because they heeded a change, they saved a life, and given the difference Jesus has made in lives ever since, they participated in the saving of millions of lives and counting!

There is returning and there is re-turning. We can stay the same and keep returning to our lives just as we've always been. Or we can, by God's help and power, re-turn. We can seek a new and different way in life. We can embrace God's power to bring about transformation and lead us to new possibilities.

One Last Thought About the Magi

One last observation is worth making. As I mentioned, the gifts the magi presented Jesus were known to have been extremely valuable. Just how much so is hard to determine, because we don't know the quantity of the gifts. However, the Bible does say they opened their treasures, as in plural. Also, near-Eastern customs would have been for people of wealth to honor a king with gestures of great significance.

Here's what we do know. Mary and Joseph were not wealthy. It is doubtful a wealthy couple would have faced their child being born in a stable. As well, when they presented Jesus at the Temple for purification as described in Luke 2, they offered a pair of turtle doves and two young pigeons. This was the offering of a poor person according to Leviticus 12:8.

When Joseph was warned in a dream to take Mary and the child and flee to Egypt to escape Herod, they would have had to live there for several years until Herod died. How did they afford to do that? Most likely they survived on the gifts of the magi. Those treasures were converted into food, clothing, and shelter. This is a good reminder of how God uses our gifts far beyond our understanding when we give them. When we give to support the cause of Christ, God uses our gifts to become life-giving, even lifesaving, resources for others.

Part of the way God re-turns us from a significant spiritual encounter is by using us to be of value in the lives of other people. What have you been given that God can use to enrich others? Have you been blessed with talents and abilities that can serve to uplift people? Do you have position and influence God might leverage to speak on behalf of people who do not have voice to represent their needs? Do you possess wealth? Have you been financially blessed in such a way that God could transform your gifts into significant lifesaving resources for others?

The God who is doing a new thing does new things in us and through us. What has God done for you and how does God want to use that?

Remember, a good return is an important key to a good journey.

Where is your Persia? What is the home where you return? If you are working, what does that world look like? What describes it? If you have a family, what does that home mean for you? What are your responsibilities? What else is in your Persia? Church or religious community? Neighborhood? Boards or committees you serve on?

If you are reading this book in Advent, you may be getting close to the end of the year. Naturally, our thoughts turn to a new year and what will be different. We may even prepare to return to our Persias with a little hesitation because of things we want to be different but fear they won't be. But don't wait for Persia to change in order to change your outlook. What is the change you can bring to your Persia? What is the compassion, energy, love, and hope you can bring to these places in your life? Places change because people change and vice versa.

When we re-turn home a different way, it's hard for home to stay the same. The way to Bethlehem changes the way from Bethlehem.

ACKNOWLEDGMENTS

I want to thank the incredible staff at Abingdon for their support and hard work in this project starting with Susan Salley with whom the idea for this resource sprouted. Though Susan is now retired, her encouragement and ideas were like a traveling companion throughout this journey. Also, I want to thank Brian Milford, president and publisher, for his confidence in me, and I especially thank Maria Mayo, an amazing editor I have had the privilege of working with now for the third time. Thank you, Maria, for your persistence, brilliance, and gentle prodding.

I am also deeply indebted to my executive assistant, Marsha Thompson, who has occupied the office next to me for eleven years. Marsha assists in research and coordination of phone calls and meetings associated with this project. She has and continues to be an answer to prayer. While I do most of my writing on days off and other personal time, there were a few periods I had to take time away from St. Luke's to complete deadlines or travel to Nashville. This makes me hugely grateful for the superb staff we have, especially our executive pastor, Jen Steulpe-Gibbs, whose outstanding leadership makes any absence of mine go unnoticed.

As well, I am immensely blessed with incredible lay leadership at St. Luke's and am thankful for their understanding and support of my time and energy going into projects like this. Finally, I am beyond grateful for my wife, Susan, who gladly stops what she's doing to read a chapter and offer suggestions. She has been my biggest cheerleader throughout our thirty-two years of ministry partnership and will be my trekking partner to the base camp of Mount Everest. Our life together has been an adventure, and the adventures continue.

NOTES

Chapter 1

1   Kiara Alfonseca, "More than 40,000 people killed in gun violence so far in 2023," ABC News, December 7, 2023, https://abcnews.go.com/ US/116-people-died-gun-violence-day-us-year/story?id=97382759.

2   "More than 50,000 Americans died by suicide in 2023—more than any year on record." Meet the Press. NBC News. December 31, 2023. https://www.nbcnews.com/meet-the-press/video/more-than-50 -000-americans-died-by-suicide-in-2023-more-than-any-year-on -record-201161285832.

3   Dean Chavers, "Before Rosa Parks, There Was Claudette Colvin," ICT News, updated September 23, 2018, https://ictnews.org/archive /before-rosa-parks-there-was-claudette-colvin.

4   Randy Maddox, ed., *The Works of John Wesley: Letters V, 1774-1781*(Nashville: Abingdon Press, 1988), 29:359.

5   Glenn MacDonald. "Open Doors." *Morning Reflections.* January 4, 2024. https://glennsreflections.com/index.php/2024/01/04/open-doors/.

6   David Williamson, "A Place of Longing," St. Luke's United Methodist Church, Indianapolis, November 26, 2017.

Chapter 2

1   Leen Ritmeyer, "Locating the Original Temple Mount," *Biblical Archeology Review*, March/April 1992, https://library.biblicalarchaeology.org/article /locating-the-original-temple-mount/.

2   Fred Craddock, *Luke: Interpretation: A Bible Commentary for Teaching and Preaching* (Louisville: Westminster John Knox Press, 2009), 22.

3   John Ortberg, *If You Want to Walk on Water, You've Got to Get Out of the Boat* (Grand Rapids: Zondervan Press, 2001), 178.

Chapter 3

1   David Herbert Donald, *Lincoln* (United Kingdom: Simon & Schuster, 2011), 29.

2   Guided tour, Epworth Rectory, Epworth, England, 2017.

3   Fred Craddock, *Luke*, 28.

4   Richard Rohr, *The Wisdom Pattern: Order, Disorder, Reorder* (Cincinnati: Franciscan Media, 2020), 136.

Chapter 4

1   Courtland Milloy, "A Poor Man Who Enriched Others' Lives," *The Washington Post*, November, 28, 2000, https://www.washingtonpost.com /archive/local/2000/11/29/a-poor-man-who-enriched-others-lives /c90104da-6ac9-4027-bfdc-a2458fde6cc5/.

2   Joyce Hollyday, "Nouns and Adverbs," *Sojourners*, March 1986, https://sojo.net/magazine/march-1986/nouns-and-adverbs.

3   Amy-Jill Levine, *The Jewish Annotated New Testament* (Oxford, UK: Oxford University Press, 2017), 101.

4   Alan Culpepper, "Luke," in *The New Interpreter's Bible,* ed. Leander E. Keck, (Nashville: Abingdon Press, 1995), 8:65.

5   Adam Hamilton, *Luke: Jesus and the Outsiders, Outcasts, and Outlaws* (Nashville: Abingdon Press, 2022), 15.

6   Richard Wilke, "Bishop's Column," *Arkansas United Methodist Reporter*, December 4, 1992, 3.

7   Quoted in Wilke, "Bishop's Column."

8   Carl Sandburg, *Remembrance Rock* (New York, Harcourt, Brace and Company, 1948), NA.

Epilogue

1   William Barclay, *The Gospel of Matthew, Volume One* (Philadelphia: Westminster John Knox Press, 1975), 26.

2   William Bridges, *Managing Transitions: Making the Most of Change, 3rd ed.* (Philadelphia: Da Capo Press, 2009), 3.

Watch videos based on *On the Way to Bethlehem: An Advent Study* with Rob Fuquay through Amplify Media.

Amplify Media is a multimedia platform that delivers high-quality, searchable content with an emphasis on Wesleyan perspectives for churchwide, group, or individual use on any device at any time. In a world of sometimes overwhelming choices, Amplify gives church leaders and congregants media capabilities that are contemporary, relevant, effective, and, most important, affordable and sustainable.

With *Amplify Media* church leaders can:

- Provide a reliable source of Christian content through a Wesleyan lens for teaching, training, and inspiration in a customizable library
- Deliver their own preaching and worship content in a way the congregation knows and appreciates
- Build the church's capacity to innovate with engaging content and accessible technology
- Equip the congregation to better understand the Bible and its application
- Deepen discipleship beyond the church walls

Ask your group leader or pastor about Amplify Media and sign up today at www.AmplifyMedia.com.